On Wings of Skye

by

Ian G. Macdonald

**Grosvenor House
Publishing Limited**

Ian G. Macdonald is hereby identified as author of this
work in accordance with Section 77 of the Copyright, Designs
and Patents Act 1988

The book cover picture is copyright to Ian G. Macdonald

This book is published by
Grosvenor House Publishing Ltd
28-30 High Street, Guildford, Surrey, GU1 3HY.
www.grosvenorhousepublishing.co.uk

A CIP record for this book
is available from the British Library

ISBN 978-1-907211-01-0

In memory of
my good friends
John Angus Matheson
and
Robert MacDonald,
far better historians than I,
who loved their native
island.

Foreword

From my earliest days I was, and am, proud to be a Skyeman and I have taken a keen interest in the History, Culture, Landscape and Natural History of my native island. I was born at Uig on 8th January 1951. Brought up in Portree, my family now live at Ollach in Braes on my great-grandfather's croft.

On the 8th of January 2006 I retired from the teaching profession after 33 years service. My final post was Depute Head Teacher at Portree High School where I had attended as a pupil from 1956 to 1969, returning as a teacher of Science and Guidance in 1980.

At the beginning of June 2006 I began to run 'On the Wing' tours for the Aros organisation based in Portree. The experience is a most enjoyable one, and led to the publication of my first book, "Like a Bird on the Wing", in the spring of 2008.

This book seems to have met with a surprising degree of appreciation from both local people and visitors alike. Friends have encouraged, and indeed persuaded, me to take a similar look at 'the other Wings of Skye'. How uplifting it has been to take a fresh interest in these other parts of my home territory. I trust that you, the reader, will derive as much pleasure from your use of this book as I have from travelling around 'The Wings', learning, re-learning and writing about them.

Enjoy!

Acknowledgments

This book, like its predecessor, is not intended as an academic work, rather a collection of observations, tales, legends and historical information, which I have picked up during my time on my native island. I hope that as, *"Like a Bird on the Wing"*, it too will be a guide to some and a stimulus to all. For those who are interested in further study and more extensive works on the subjects touched on, I have included a list of some of the best books on Skye, and related topics, which will satisfy even the most demanding and studious. All of those included in the list have been of benefit to me.

I extend many thanks to those who, wittingly, or unwittingly, have helped me with this effort.

My former teachers at Portree High, George Moody, Alistair Turner, Forrest Moffat and especially the late Robin Murray who ran the School Field Club, which first gave me an insight into the wonderful scenery and wildlife that Skye has to offer. From these scientists and geographers I learned much of what appears in these pages.

Any book about events in the Highlands has to rely to some extent on *'Beul-aithris nan seanar'* ('the tradition of the elders', folktales, or unwritten history). Some tales in these pages I learned as a boy and therefore have no means of verifying; other tales were told me second-hand in good faith and yet others I have read and now revamp.

No booklet or indeed article, about the Isle of Skye should be contemplated until one has read Alexander Nicolson's classic *"History of Skye"* and Alexander Cameron's *"The History and Traditions of the Isle of Skye"*.

Many thanks go to my former primary school teacher, Christine MacLean, for proofreading and correcting my spelling and punctuation. Any further mistakes which remain, were probably inserted later, and are my own! Thanks to Cailean Maclean for his encouragement and advice; to Christine Thomson, Charles MacLeod, John Gillies, John Angus MacKenzie, Mary Ann MacFarlane, Ann Nicolson, Murdo Beaton, Harry MacArthur, Donald Macdonald, Alister Ross, David McClymont, the ladies at *Dualchas*, Ann MacLeod, Alison Beaton, Emily MacDonald and Nanette Muir for their knowledgeable input and research. Your help is much appreciated.

Finally, and most importantly, I acknowledge with gratitude the superlative beauty of the landscape through which we travel. Even when the weather is indifferent, the views are sometimes astounding. Having myself travelled widely in Europe, I know of nowhere else with such appealing topography. When we park at the viewpoint at Rigg, and passengers from all parts of the World gasp with astonishment at the vista before them, I am reminded that we should indeed be grateful, not only for our wonderful surroundings but for the health and capacity, both physical and mental, to enjoy them.

I G M

Wings of Skye

"Do sgiathan àlainn air an lùbadh
Mu Loch Bhràcadail ioma-
chùilteach,
Do sgiathan bòidheach ri muir
sleuchdte
Bho 'n Eist Fhiadhaich gu Aird
Shléite,
Do sgiathan aoibhneach air an
sgaoileadh
Mu Loch Shnigheasort is mun
t-saoghal."

Dr Sorley MacLean

"Your supremely beautiful wings
bent
About many-nooked Loch
Bracadale,
Your beautiful wings prostrate on
the sea
From the Wild Stallion to the Aird
of Sleat,
Your joyous wings spread
About Loch Snizort and the
World."

5

CHAPTER 1

Portree
Thoughts from the Golf Course

My previous book, 'Like a Bird on the Wing', took us from Portree around the wing of Skye called Trotternish, via Staffin, Duntulm and Uig before returning to the Island's capital. In this second journey, we set off from Portree to Vaternish, in the direction of 'The Great North Road', as it is described by Canon MacCulloch in his book, 'The Misty Isle of Skye', first published in 1905.

MacCulloch continues; "The pleasure of the highway will depend much on the weather. I have travelled across it when the whole atmosphere seemed a mere blinding sheet of water, and, over the undulating moorland and down the sides of the hills, the wind swept unceasingly and lashed itself into fury. But there are days when it shows to better advantage, when the mysterious moorland and the winding sea-lochs by which it wanders and the glimpses of the distant islands and glimmering horizons, enchant the wayfarer."

Memories of my childhood suggest, probably wrongly, that the latter was much more common in the 1950s and 60s.

Be that as it may, during the entire month of May 2008 the weather was so glorious that to travel this road to Vaternish was a sheer joy and privilege. Nowadays, we have the choice to walk, cycle or motor on the 'Great North Road', but in 1840 the Rev. A. Clark of Duirinish wrote: "for some years after the construction of the road, the common people would not on any account,

7

travel on it as the stones and gravel bruised their bare feet." They preferred the boggy and well-trodden paths of their forefathers.

On leaving Portree we will first set out on an interesting by-way, the B885 known locally as the *Hill Road*. As young lads, growing up in *Portree*, we spent many of the warm sunny days of the summer holidays on, what was then, the small nine-hole golf course. My friend, John Angus Matheson, was greenkeeper as well as an outstanding young golfer. Those were joyous days listening to the singing of the skylarks, tutting of wheatears and the mewing of buzzards.

What better place than the former third green of the golf course for us now to sit awhile, as *Màiri Mhòr nan Òran* did, look over *Portree*, and muse upon pleasant memories and the historical happenings which this place has witnessed.

"Suidh air cnocan uain'	Sit on a green hillock
Air Cruachan Saidhebhinn,	On Cruachan Saidhebhinn,
Seall gach taobh mun cuairt dut	Look all round about you
Eadar cuan is tìr."	Between both sea and land.

During school time we also ventured out here with our Science Teacher Robin Murray. He was, undoubtedly, a pioneer of learning through practical experience. He began with what to us sounded like a bizarre suggestion. *"Do you think we could produce enough hydro-electricity from the Mill Burn to power the school in term time?"* We calculated height, flow-rate, average water level, energy produced, efficiency, potential sites for a mini power-station and eventually concluded that it would indeed be possible to power, not only the school, but also both school hostels all year round from this little stream! Robin opened for us a new window on a wider World, while at the same time fostering a growing appreciation of the unique wonder which we had on our own doorstep. The Mill Dam and Mill Pond, haunts of dragonflies and lacewings, were a source of tadpoles, and an introduction to our love of wildlife. The original purpose of the outflow from the dam was to drive the belts and wheels in the Wool and Saw mills and to provide clean water for scouring the wool.

In the 1880s the Wool Mill was operated by the Border firm of Hogg Woollen Mills and was visited by a Lady MacAskill of Skye descent. She considered that the workers were poorly paid and were being exploited. When Malcolm Ferguson visited in 1882 he was much more enthusiastic as considerable employment was being provided for the poor in the village. At that time some Glasgow engineers were putting in a new 30hp steam engine to assist the water wheel. By the 1960s, the Saw Mill was diesel powered and the Wool Mill, having been through the experience of the revolution of James Watt's steam engine, was now a modern factory, operated since 1945 by James Pringle and his two sons, William and Hamish. In 1970 a new company Skye Wool Mills Ltd. was formed.

Robin traced for us the skilfully fashioned aquifers and channels which tapped the hill streams below the golf course, fed the Dam and negotiated the Margaret Carnegie Hostel to provide the force which had formerly driven their machinery.

Nowadays, the Pond remains as an extension to the Biology Labs of the New *Portree* High School but the Dam has gone. It is replaced by *Pàirc na Laoch,* the Field of Heroes, where the shinty teams of *Skye Camanachd* and the local schools do battle with mainland opponents and, young people, once again, learn the skills and joys of this sport. Dr. Sorley MacLean regarded shinty as the Chief of Sports. His poem *An t-Earrach 1937* (Spring 1937) speaks of the hardy and courageous boys who played for *Portree* School in the Robertson Cup final, some of them losing their lives, but all losing the joy of youth in the World War that was shortly to follow.

Latha o chionn lethchiad bliadhna,	A day fifty years ago,
Latha grianach ciuin,	A calm sunny day,
Gun snaithnean ceotha air a'	Without a thread of mist on the Cuillin
Chuilthionn	Or on the skull of the Storr.
No air claigeann a'Stoir.	
Ach an diugh ceo eile	But today another mist
Air raon mor na Borlainn,	On the big Home Farm field,
Ceo na lathaichean a dh'fhalbh	Mist of the days that have gone,
Ciar thar na h-oigridh a chaill an	Dim over the youth that have lost their
oige	youth,
Is ochdnar dhen da-dhiag marbh.	And eight of the twelve dead.

In our young days the Golf Course was shared with a flock of blackface sheep, owned and herded by Calum MacLeod and his skilful team of five border-collie dogs. His day-job was with the Hydro Board. With a subtlety which hinted at our local and literary knowledge we called him "The Electric Shepherd!"

Beneath us lies *Shulishader* farmhouse. I remember the hay coils and corn stooks which filled the fertile fields of late summer. The farmer was Roderick Nicolson (*Ruaraidh Mòr Shulishaidir*) who seemed to us to be such a big strong man, except on the day he hurried into the ladies' staffroom in the school with blood pouring freely from his hand. While working on his field at *Seafield,* he had caught his finger in a machine for sowing grain. We later learned that he had lost most of one finger. As ghoulish young lads, we ever after sought to get a glimpse of his hand to see the damage that had been inflicted that day. The accident, however, did not hinder his diligent crofting in any way and he continued, like so many others of that generation, to work hard to make a living and keep his land in good heart.

Then there was the day of the Cross Country Championships. Farquhar MacLean, Principal Teacher of PE, gave us our route and set us off. Up by the 'pigs' walk' at *Viewfield* to the white strainer-post in the forestry fence, then due north towards the golf course and back to school via the hostel road and the woods behind the school. All should have been straight forward, and progress, for most of the route, could be followed by the teacher with binoculars, from the sports' pitch. Duncan Geddes from the Isle of Soay had other ideas. He took a shortcut across one of Ruaraidh's ploughed fields and was spotted. Within the hour, the burly crofter was in the school office without the courtesy of a knock, demanding suitable punishment for the lad and the teacher responsible. Farquhar was called and explained that Alistair Douglas was in charge of cross-country running and Ruaraidh should take the matter up with him. Mr Douglas, the teacher of Technical Subjects, had nothing whatever to do with the incident, and was in fact safely at a meeting in Inverness on that particular day!

From the old Golf Course we look back to the ever-growing village of *Portree* and the salmon farm beyond the black rock at the mouth of the harbour. Changed days from when the cobles emptied the bag-nets of wild Atlantic salmon twice a day, six days per week. In the 1880s, eighty eight men were employed, from May to October, between *Portree* and *Staffin* in this business and the fish were stored in the ice-house at the bottom of *Quay Brae* ready for their journey to the tables of the best city restaurants. The ice was taken by cart or lorry from the ice dam at *Sluggans* during wintry weather. This was still common practice in my young days. We must have had much colder winters then! Not much snow and ice nowadays! Is this global warming at work or just part of an ever-changing pattern?

The earliest mention that I have found of *Portree's* ice-house is a reference in 1832 to James Gillespie-Graham having oversight of it as part of his duties as Clerk of Works to Lord MacDonald. Only in 1952, with the coming of electricity from the *Storr* Hydro-electric power-station was an ice-making plant installed at the *Quay Brae* site.

The corner of the ice-house on *Quay Brae* was one of four places in the village where, at the turn of the 19th to 20th

Century, street-lights were allowed to burn all night. There was another light at the top of the hill on *Armadale House* and two others in *Somerled Square*. The other 33 street-lights were extinguished at 11pm by Donald (Disher) Nicolson the lamplighter. These lamps were oil burners and required to be filled every second evening. The lights extended out to the *Bridge*, up *Stormy Hill* and out *Staffin Road*; i.e. where 'the quality' lived.

But what other significant harbour events might have been viewed from our 'Golf Course' spot by the former inhabitants of *Kiltaraglen* and *Portree* over the years? Perhaps in 585AD they would have witnessed the Irish Saint Columba and his followers come ashore on the little island in the bay and set up the little chapel which is still named for him. He and his followers were first to bring Christianity to the West of Scotland.

In the month of September1263, the locals might have observed the vast fleet of King *Haakon* of Norway sweeping south under full sail through the *Sound of Raasay* to *Kyleakin* (Kyle Haakon) and thence to defeat by Alexander III of Scotland at the Battle of Largs. Haakon's own longboat was of great dimensions, built entirely of oak, and ornamented with richly carved dragons, overlaid with gold which would doubtless have reflected the rays of the autumn sun. He had sailed from Norway in July and had travelled via Lewis and North Skye where he had added greatly to his fleet. More than a hundred galleys sailed past this spot and we know that one of them was commanded by an Andrew Nicolson of *Trotternish*. Skye's oldest Clan, the Nicolsons, are said to have taken possession of *Scorrybreck* and *Lonfearn* in 950AD.

At *Kyleakin*, the King was joined by a further fleet of petty chiefs, as well as Magnus King of Man who was destined to be Haakon's successor, and to sign the Treaty of Perth in 1266 in which the Norse gave up all claim to the Scottish islands. It is also interesting to note that another Nicolson fought, this time, on the winning side! John Muldovie Nicolson was rewarded by King Alexander. He it was who built the first *Scorrybreck House.*

In 1540 King James V of Scotland stepped ashore here at *Creag na Mòr Sluagh* (the Rock of the Multitude) to be guest of the Nicolson Chief at *Scorrybreck* House. Doubtless, there would have been great fear among the inhabitants of *Port Righ,* the King's Harbour, as his army spread out to encamp all around the bay. The Chiefs of Clan MacLeod and Clan MacDonald were summoned to attend the King's Court and to pledge their allegiance to his person.

Not until the 1830s would such a large fleet be seen from here again.

The Rev. Coll Macdonald, writing in the *New Statistical Account,* says that a company of south-countrymen was formed at *Portree* to cure fish (including salmon) and send them by steamer to Glasgow and thence to London. He went on to say:

"*The herring fishing, some years ago, was carried on here with considerable success. In a fine evening in the month of July or August when all the boats belonging to this parish (Portree) and the adjacent parishes of Glenelg, Lochalsh, Lochcarron, Applecross, Gairloch, and Loch Broom ... from fifty to seventy sail in number, appeared in the Sound of Raasay, a most delightful scene was exhibited. But the most agreeable and most useful of all exhibitions was their return to the harbour the next day, deeply laden with the richest and most delicious herrings.*"

There was nothing agreeable about the emigrant ships and little joy as they sailed off from here carrying a people to the farthest corners of the earth. What sadness there would be as these vessels cleared the harbour to the plaintive sounds of a Gaelic Psalm taken up by the passengers and by their loved ones on the Black Rock.

"When the bold kindred, in the time long-vanished,
Conquered the soil and fortified the keep—
No seer foretold the children would be banished,
That a degenerate lord might boast his sheep:
Fair these broad meads, these hoary woods are grand;
But we are exiles from our fathers' land."

On 12th September 1773, Johnson and Boswell came into the harbour. *"Raasay has a stout boat, built in Norway, in which, with six oars, he conveyed us back to Sky. We landed at Port Re. The port is made by an inlet of the sea, deep and narrow, where a ship lay (the Nestor), waiting to dispeople Sky, by carrying the natives away to America."*

But over the years there would often be local interest generated as individual commercial vessels sailed back and fore to and from this harbour.

The first recorded steamship sailing to Skye was the paddle steamer *Highlander* in 1822. In 1827 *Maid of Morven* came here from Oban via Tobermory and by 1846, the steamers *Shandon, Dolphin* and *Tartar* were sailing regularly from Glasgow to Ardrishaig, Oban, Tobermory and *Portree* and *Mary Jane* began her trips from Glasgow to Stornoway, calling in at *Portree*. Some years later *Duntroon Castle* plied the route from Oban. *Chevalier* began sailing here in 1853. Of the above, *Mary Jane*, which had made her first voyage on 18 June 1846, had the longest lifespan. In 1875 her name was changed to *Glencoe*. It was from the *Glencoe* that Sheriff Ivory and fifty Glasgow Policemen disembarked on 6th April 1882, the day prior to the *Battle of the Braes*, often heralded as "the last battle on British soil". In 1918 she became the regular mailboat to Portree and continued on the route until May 1931. Another well known name was the *SS Lochiel*, which in the 1880s and 1890s plied the *Portree, Tarbert, Lochmaddy and Dunvegan* circuit. In fact, she ended her career in 1907 by running aground at *Portree*. Of the other steamers which serviced this part of Skye, we should also mention the *SS Gael*,

SS Plover, SS Clydesdale and *SS Sheila* as they became household names. *SS Sheila,* named after a character in William Black's tale *"A Princess of Thule"*, acquired a reputation in bad weather. A potential passenger on *Portree* pier was heard to say to his companion, *"Here comes the Sheila, I'm sick already!"*

In our young days, the *Loch Nevis* and the *Loch Arkaig* were the passenger vessels sailing to *Raasay, Kyle* and *Mallaig*, the latter captained by my friend Iain's father, Lachlan MacRae. These passenger vessels conducted locals and visitors alike to and from the nearest railheads and were a lifeline until the the road network was improved. The 'steamers' would sail from the pier at a very early hour of the morning, and this prompted J F Marshall to pen his delightful poem 'Out of Skye';

"A lamp-lit quay that glitters in the rain,
And by its side a steamboat waiting dawn,
A flock of sheep with shepherds following on,
Some tourists, heavy-eyed, then sleep again –
Hoarse cries are heard; the silly sheep are fain
To double on the gangway and be gone.
No help: the dogs are on them, and anon
They're penned on deck, still bleating, but in vain.
The daylight strengthens, and the sirens sound;
The last rope splashes, and the engines churn;
The quayside fades. O misty isle, it seems
As if no time to leave thee could be found
More fitting than the the hour in which men turn
From sleeping, and, reluctant, lose their dreams."

On Saturdays, the *Loch Dunvegan* called with cargo from the Clyde – tea-chests of groceries and bags of seed potatoes from MacFarlane Shearer of Greenock. What joy we had as children, anticipating the riches in these boxes! In fact, even the empty tea-chests served as our playthings as we re-enacted 'pirate times' or made 'houses'.

On Sunday 17th November 1846 it was warships that entered the Bay. *HMS Assistance* and *HMS Forester* accompanied by the *Lochiel* had come to quell the Crofter agitation with a force of marines and policemen. *"The appearance of warships in the bay of Portree did not visibly disturb the good people of the town. They looked upon the expedition from the purely commercial point of view, but it was a failure in this respect"* wrote James Cameron. Sixteen pressmen and two artists had also travelled to Skye. They exposed in the National Papers the collusion of the Landlords, Judiciary and Military in suppressing the crofters' struggle. *"The publicity of the brutal details of the raid on Herbusta excited, not only at home but in Canada and Australia, feelings of disgust against a government that could permit such unholy things being done in its name,"* continued Cameron. Undoubtedly, it was publicity of this kind which speeded up the preparation of legislation for the Crofters' Holdings Act of 1886 which finally gave security of tenure to the crofters of the Highlands and Islands.

Portree Bay and its visiting vessels have certainly been to the fore in the History of Scotland.

Near us, as we continue our musings from the Golf Course, is the former Ross Memorial Fever Hospital, lately used as the *An Tuireann Arts Centre* which has exhibited some excellent artwork, including the wonderful Skye paintings of Dutch artist Fred Schley. Fred has been visiting Skye for more than twenty years and is captivated by the light and landscape. His interest in the island, its people and its history has also expressed itself in two fine portraits of the Skye poets *Màiri Mhòr nan Òran* and Dr. Sorley MacLean. The first of these was commissioned by Highland Council after Fred had kindly gifted Sorley's portrait to them.

When we were young, the old Fever Hospital was a consulting area for the affable Physiotherapist, Angus Robertson. My brother attended for some weeks following a football injury and received excellent treatment from that courteous gentleman.

In the early years of the 20th century, the isolation unit at the Ross Memorial Hospital proved very useful from time to time. The school log for October 1904 tells us that there was, "A whooping cough scare in the village — not many cases but families are afraid."

In February 1910, there was an outbreak of diphtheria and a family of five was taken in for isolation. In fact, in a severe case of scarlet fever in 1914 the school was closed from September to December and the Christmas Holiday was cancelled to make up for the loss of schooling time!

The hospital was built in 1891 in memory of Dr. David Ross M.D., who single-handedly nursed his typhoid patients through 1887. He himself succumbed to the disease and died at Beaumont House on 24th December of that year. This man was certainly a hero of his profession!

We have already made mention of the Margaret Carnegie building which is situated below us. Prior to 1924, it was the local Poor House, built in 1860, but was purchased for £3000 by the Trustees of the Carnegie UK Trust, as a school hostel for girls, and named after the daughter of its founder Andrew Carnegie. Two similar buildings were also purchased in *Stornoway*, one for boys and one for girls. By 1930, it was judged that these hostels had been so successful that the Trust was determined to have a specially constructed boys' hostel built in *Portree*. Mr James Shearer, advising architect to the Trust, designed the beautiful Elgin Hostel, named after the 10th Earl of Elgin and 14th of Kirkcardine who was now the Trust chairman. Situated beside the school, on land granted by the MacDonald Estates, the Elgin Hostel was opened on Tuesday 12th September 1933 by Their Highnesses The Duke and Duchess of York. (He was later to become George VI and she is better known as the late Queen Mother.)

It's interesting that the menu for lunch on that day consisted only of local produce but indeed fit for a king!

Herrings Fried in Oatmeal
Roast Lobster

Cold Lamb ò Rowan Jelly
Cold Grouse ò Snipe Cream
Potatoes in Jackets
Carrageen Mould

Curds with Cream
Apple Tartlets
Raspberry Mousse

Crowdie and Oatcakes

Coffee

The Duke was resplendent in Highland Dress of Stuart Tartan and the Duchess wore a blue coat and hat. She also wore a silver grey fox fur, which today would not be politically correct, but then demand meant that fox trappers were getting one whole shilling for Renard's brush!

The press reported that, *"The weather was dull with Portree shrouded in mist. However, it cleared later and remained fine."*

In his speech, the Duke referred to Skye as, "The isle of kind and loyal hearts."

We are told that the building sand for this superb edifice was shipped across Portree Bay from *Camus Bàn* by Donald Nicolson's Family (the Dishers of Bayfield). They were required to off-load it at the top of the old slipway and received one shilling per bag. This was regarded as good pay. Horse and cart were then used to convey it to the site. The salt content of this sea-sand does not seem to have had any adverse effect on the walls of the Elgin Hostel, but perhaps it was required to be well washed before use.

Over the years, these hostels became the home-from-home of countless school pupils from around Skye and several of the neighbouring islands and, if these buildings could speak, they would have lots of tales to tell.

An interesting feature of the Elgin Hostel was the tradition of nicknames given ceremonially to the 'new boys'. From my own youth, I remember *'Volt'* who became high-powered in the Gaelic Cause. *'Fingers'* is a Church of Scotland minister. *'Ham'* and *'Ping'* are senior managers in education, *'Tango'* is also a high-flyer. A pilot! — and *'Toggle'* pedals drugs on Wentworth Street! (Local pharmacist)

Ann MacKinnon's poem from the 1964-65 school magazine reflected on these names in Chaucer-speak! Just a few lines will whet the appetite.

'A **Lamb** ther was and that a worthy beast
And of the prefects he was nat the least.
With ladies fair he practised chivalrye
Most oft with on y'named as Chrissye.
The cloak he wered was of deep maroon
With golde braid around his habergeoun.
He was a verray parfit gentil knight
N'er lit a fag till skool was out of sight.

A **Skate** from Raasay also for the nones
Ful thin he was of face and eek of bones
His face as any sow or fox was reed
To classes in the skool he payed no heed
A skool-bel wel coude he ring and soune
With Maggie from Glendale he walked the toune.
He was ungrounded in astronomye
But learned was in campanologye."

Both these gents became well known in later life as respected professionals on the island!

Above *Shulishader*, the hill is *Aite Suidhe Fhinn* or Fingal's Seat, where it is said the Irish giant-hero used to sit while directing his deerhounds *Bran* and *Fraoch* and his followers, the *Feinne* or Fingalians, as they hunted the deer on the *Mointeach Mor* below. Skye's first native writer, Martin Martin, in his book published in 1716, speaks highly of *Fionn* or Fingal. *"A kind friend, an adviser of judgement, wise in counsel, able to solve doubts and difficulties, hospitable to all, ever ready to protect the weak and defenceless".*

"The door of Fionn is always open, and the name of his hall is the stranger's home."

There is a Gaelic saying still in common use:
"Cha deachaidh neach riamh Dubhach bho Fhionn", "None ever went sad from Fionn."

How relevant then for the New *Portree* High School Community facilities to be named *'Àrainn Fhinn'* or 'The Fingal Centre'.

Of the individual Fingalian, Martin says; *"He must be light and swift so as not to break a rotten branch by standing on it, he must leap a tree as high as his forehead and get under a tree no higher than his knee: without stopping he must be able to draw a thorn from his foot."*

On Skye's annual Games Day, the Hill Race runners, worthy successors to the *Feinne*, set out from the *Meall*, cross the bay at low tide to *Fisherfield* and ascend to the escarpment above the woodland beneath *Fingal's Seat*. On reaching the checkpoint they make their best way back to the Games Field to the acclaim of the large crowd. For this they require stout hearts and strong legs.

The first ever Skye Games were held on Thursday 6th September 1877, not at *The Lump* (*Meall na h-Acarsaid*), as nowadays, but at the *Home Farm Field*, (*Air raon mor na Borlainn*). In August this year, 2008, the event celebrated its 131st year and the occasion has only been interrupted by World Wars.

In 1892, the Skye Gathering Committee bought a piece of ground at *'Fancy Hill'* or *'The Lump'* as a permanent home for the Games competitions. The Inverness Courier called this *"a picturesque site, which commands a fine view of the harbour; indeed, not only a fine view but a commanding view, for a gun could be placed upon it so as to defeat half-a-dozen of the finest ships of any navy."*

By 1893 part of the rock had been blasted from 'The Lump' to make a fine amphitheatre to host a running track and arena for caber tossing, hammer throwing and various other 'heavy' field events. The surrounding area provided for an audience of up to 5000 people. While the most important events at the Games have always been the Piping and Highland Dancing Competitions, over the years there have been other attractions – a well attended regatta for the yachts of the 'nobility' and the skiffs and rowboats of the 'commoners', a cycle race, trips on the flying-boat *'Cloud of Iona'* and of course the annual tug-of-war event.

The Skye Games continued into the 20th Century and, apart from the war years, were held annually in the month of August. In 1950, in the hope that visitors would be attracted to the island earlier in the year, Skye Week was instituted in the month of May. As part of this, a second Highland Games were held. The practice continued well into the 1970s but, even after Skye Week was dropped, the annual August event continued, and has flourished. Over the years there have been days of brilliant weather and, on occasions, more challenging conditions! The Skye Midges certainly have the day pencilled into their calendar and much tourist blood is drawn!

When weather permitted, the open piping competitions for youngsters were held at the Apothecary's Tower which overlooks Portree Pier. Built by the famous Dr Alexander MacLeod (*An Dotair Ban*), the prominent tower served the purpose of informing sailing ships of the presence of medical services in the village. At one time the tower is believed to have been used as a dispensary. The *Dotair Ban* was born in North Uist in 1788. He graduated from Edinburgh University in 1809 in Anatomy, Surgery and Pharmacy. His vast knowledge and skills led to his appointment as Chamberlain of Estates to Lord

MacDonald and to his living in Portree from 1829 to 1835. He laid out *'Fancy Hill'* to be pleasure gardens for the village. He is fondly remembered in Skye, both for his many public works and his sense of humour. While acting as Factor he never charged for his medical services. It was said of him *"he was probably the most popular man who ever acted in that capacity in the Highlands"*. On one occasion he diagnosed a lady as suffering from indigestion, indolence and excessive drinking of black tea. He ordered her to drink a large cup of milk while sitting on a stone outside her house. She was then to climb the 400 foot hill behind the village and, facing east, inhale ten deep breaths. This was to be repeated morning and evening and 'no tea'. She believed her 'cure' was due to 'the breaths from the east'.

He firmly believed in the health-giving properties of dulse and shellfish and Mary MacPherson has captured this in her well known verses.

Ach cuimhnichibh, a luchd mo gràidh,	But remember my loved ones',
Comhairlean an Dotair Bhàin,	The advice of the Doctor Ban,
Thugaibh pailteas as an tràigh,	Take plenty from the seashore,
Is deanabh cal air deanntaig.	And make soup of nettles.
'S o'n a dh'fhalbh an Dotair Bàn,	Since the fair Doctor departed,
Cha bhi duil againn gu bràth,	We will never again expect,
Ri fear sheasas-dhuinn 'na àit,	Anyone to fill his place,
Ach's math am plàsd a chainnt dhuinn.	But his words are good medicine for us.

To the south and on the same level as the old Golf Course is *Viewfield* House (*Taigh Ghoirtean na Creige*) which was the home, of the redoubtable Colonel Jock MacDonald. Jock was a much loved and witty character who, in my young days, was often seen around Portree wearing a threadbare kilt of the suitably named Ancient MacDonald tartan. Born in 1889, Jock attended Portree Primary School but went on to Fettes College, Edinburgh for his secondary education. Although while there he took up rugby and won a cap for Scotland, shinty was his great love. Jock became a tea planter and also served for a time in the Indian Army; he and his wife returned to Skye after World War II. His Gaelic, of which he was extremely proud, was as fluent as when he had left Skye as a youth. Immensely keen on piping, and no mean player himself, he was a stalwart of the Highland Games and encouraged local players at ceilidhs held at his home.

There are many tales told of the Colonel and his eccentric animals!

Ossie, the live owl, was often put into one of the large cases of stuffed birds which so impress visitors to *Viewfield*. While examining the specimens, one would become aware of a sudden movement or blink of an eye causing startled exclamations on the visitor's part and loud guffaws from Jock and Evelyn!

At one time, he had a large deerhound which followed him everywhere. My brother Duncan was Colour Sergeant in the local Army Cadet Force and had occasion to call at *Viewfield* to present a bill in connection with some event. The dog ate the invoice and the fivers which Jock had laid on the table!

Jock was often to be seen driving around *Portree* with tractor and trailer collecting food scraps from the local hotels for his pigs.

I'm indebted to my friend and former colleague Murdo Beaton for the following tale from his article on the Portree High School website.

"I will close with an account of an incident that took place during my 6th year at school and which will live in my memory for the rest of my life. I was called out of class one day along with two others - Murdo Gillies and Alasdair MacLeod - and told to report to the Headmaster, at that time Iain M Murray. Col Jock MacDonald of Viewfield was in the office with the headmaster and we were asked if we would go and assist the Colonel with a little task. Thus started one of the most hilarious escapades I have ever been involved in. We were taken to Viewfield House in Jock's car with his collie dogs licking the back of our necks and the windscreen wipers going at full speed even though it was a bright, sunny summer's day. When we arrived we were greeted by the sight of several very large pigs lying dead here and there - one was on the lawn in front of the house and another was in the rhododendron bushes at the side of the drive. We had to drag them to a large hole in the back garden which

Jock had already dug - they had apparently escaped for the umpteenth time that morning and Jock had, in exasperation, solved the problem by shooting them. The last one to be dragged unceremoniously to her last resting place was the one from the bushes at the side of the drive and every now and then when we stopped for a rest Jock would mutter sadly, "Seonaid bhochd, Seonaid bhochd!" When we had completed the task and were standing admiring our handiwork the Colonel looked across at us and said "A Pheutanaich, bho'n is tu's coltaiche ri minisdear, nach can thu facal!" 'Beaton, as you are the one most like a minister, say a few words!"'

As an old man, while attending a local funeral, Jock was heard to say to another octogenarian; "*Saoil an fhiach dhuinn a dhol dhachaidh a seo?*" "Is it really worth our while going home?"

Jock was for many years, until his death in 1980, chieftain of the Skye Highland Games and Skye Camanachd.

But it's now time to resume our journey to join '*The Great North Road*' of MacCulloch's book and head towards the wings of the west. As we make our way back to the *Hill Road*, a skylark is singing joyfully above, reminding us that we have the prospect of this delightful day continuing fine.

'*N uiseag air a sgiath,*	Skylark on the wing,
Seinn gun fhiamh a ciùil,	Sings it's uninhibited song,
'*S an ceò mu cheann Beinn Tionabhaig,*	The head-mist on Ben Tianavaig,
Is an sliabh fo dhriùchd.	And the moor bedecked with dew.

They say that when a skylark is threatened by a raptor it simply flies higher and sings louder. Perhaps there is a message there for us, when in adversity!

CHAPTER 2

Woodend Views

We set off again on the *Hill Road*, through the birch and hazel woods, as the blue *Storr* mountain peeps out above the lesser brown hills to the east. This side of the valley provides us with several vantage points from which we can look over *Sluggans* to *Craigleadh* and the meandering *River Leasgeary*.

It was in a deep pool in this stream, *The Target*, where a previous generation of *Portree* youngsters learned to swim. My own generation had the advantage of being taught by the redoubtable Annie Weir in her canvas pool! Mrs Weir began her lessons on dry land. We learned the rudiments of the breast-stroke lying belly-down on the gym benches! Once the theory was mastered, we graduated to the very cold water. Any nonsense was quickly stemmed with the threat of "a pink skin" from her ever-present sandshoe. Annie had been very concerned at the fact that most West Coast fishermen could not swim and there had been several drownings. It was due to her almost single-handed efforts that *Portree* eventually got a purpose-built Swimming Pool. How fitting that her name is commemorated in the lovely new facility at *Portree* High School.

Strung out to the right are the townships of *Torvaig* and *Achachork* where the modern houses of *Portree's* suburbs stand shoulder to shoulder with croft houses, polytunnels and agricultural sheds. *Achachork* means 'field of corn', not the corn of the American and Canadian prairies which many Skyemen came to know; but oats which formed the staple diet of the indigenous people here for hundreds of years. It is not without significance that oats appear twice on the menu for the Elgin Hostel opening! I remember well my grandfather's love for *stapag*, rich cream with toasted oatmeal mixed in. He would be assured of a glass from the Macintoshes at *Kiltaraglen*, whom he always visited on his annual, 'Fair fortnight' summer holiday from the Clyde Shipyards.

It was said by Dean Monro, writing in 1549 that Skye was famous *'both for the abundance and excellence'* of its oat crop. Again, Martin Martin, writing of the late 1600s says, *"I have an account that a small tract of ground in Scorrybreck yielded one hundredfold barley,"* and in the 18th Century a visiting Captain Burt states; *"every available patch was cultivated by the (crooked) spade, and crops of oats and barley were grown".*

These crops, much despised in years of affluence, but now beginning to feature in haute (or oat) cuisine and healthy diets, were of major significance to our clansmen, sustaining them as they followed their chiefs on lengthy campaigns through Scotland; to Flodden, Worchester and Derby in England and on voyages to wars in Ireland, relying only on *fuarag eòrna,* barley meal.

History looks back in astonishment at the long forced marches of Montrose's campaigns when his Highland army subsisted on a little oatmeal and cold water and slept in all weathers clad only in the *breacan feile,* (the one-piece kilt and plaid).

Angus MacRuary, owner of 'The Isle of Skye Brewery', tells me that he hopes to grow barley at *Bornesketaig* for brewing purposes. The last Skye crops were grown in the late 1950s or early 60s. If he can perfect the cultivation of a dwarf variety of hops in a polytunnel, the full product will be 'made in Skye with only Skye ingredients'.

We are told that there were three methods by which the grain could be prepared for milling: parching in a kiln, *ealachaidh,* parching in a pot over the fire, *earraraidh* and *gradaning,* in which the sheaves of corn were held over the fire and the ears were separated from the straw and partially parched before grinding. This latter method was particularly wasteful as much of the straw became burnt, singed or generally unusable. As usual, Dr Johnson had something to say on the subject; "*With the genuine improvidence of savages, they destroy the fodder for the want of which their cattle perish*". Gradaning was banned on the MacDonald Estates from 1765.

An old poem mentions all three methods.

"*Ma 's ealachaidh a th'agad, no gradan,* *Ma 's earraraidh e, thoir dhomh màm;* '*S ma's acras, gu'r manadh 'ga chasgadh,* *Fideadann blasda mhin bhàin.*"	"Whether the grain be parched in a pot or by flame, Whether in the kiln, give me a bag; If you suffer from hunger the means of arresting it, Are the tasty crumbs of white meal."

The straw had another important use as thatch for the houses. Having served that purpose, it would be taken off the roof on a fine spring day and, with its thick coat of soot from the central cooking-fire, would then be recycled as fertiliser for the next season's crop. Cattle manure and seaweed also helped to restore fertility to the soil, but the constant re-use of the same rigs led to poorer and poorer yields.

The introduction of potatoes around 1750 was a welcome life-saver but the people came to rely on this crop too much, so that in the years when the potatoes failed, starvation was the inevitable result. 1835 and 1836 were known as The Destitution Years, due to poor harvests, when most crops suffered. By 1841, a total of 32,000 barrels of potatoes were grown in this parish alone, so that we can appreciate that the Potato Famine of 1845 had a devastating effect on the population here, as it did elsewhere in the British Isles.

In the 16th Century, the rental for a penny-land or *fearann peighinn* in these townships was "*6 stones of meal, 6 stones of cheese,*

1 cow and eke in money 4s 2d". Twenty penny-lands were equal to the *tirunga* or *ounceland*. Even the penny-land was often subdivided to *lephin* or half penny and *feorling* or farthing land. *Merkland* was quarter land or equal to five penny-lands. On our journey we will pass through townships named *Lephin* and *Feorlig* as well as several beginning *Peigh-* or *Pein-*. Indeed, the townships of *Woodend*, *Glengrasco*, *Uigishadder* and *Peiness*, through which we are now passing, are part of *Ung na Cille*, the ounce land of the church.

Between *Woodend* and *Achachork* is the *Mointeach Mòr* or big moss. This area was once the main fuel supplier for *Portree*. Large quantities of peat were cut to keep the home fires burning. Peat has roughly 50% of the calorific value of coal and is a relatively clean fuel which leaves very little ash. It is a renewable energy source but the peat is replaced only very slowly, as each year's vegetation grows over that of the previous year. This is the reason why commercial peat extraction for gardens and power stations is now frowned upon in EC circles; other than Eire! The boggy acid conditions only suit certain plants, so the area is regarded as dull, brown and uninteresting by some, but actually ideal territory for insects and amphibians. William MacKenzie in his, *"Traditions, Reflections and Memories,"* refers to it as *"a blot on the landscape which could easily be drained and reclaimed into pasture land"*. Contrast this comment with 21st Century statements from spokespersons for Scottish National Heritage!

As young lads we discussed the possibility of building an airstrip here, close to Skye's capital, but the debate was won by *Ashaig* near *Broadford*, due to the significant differences in cost that would be incurred in excavating the peat, compared to simply levelling a coastal strip. Unfortunately, the *Ashaig* Airstrip itself has come to very little, due to lack of investment. Opening in April 1972, commercial flights continued until 1988.

It was on the *Mointeach* that the cattle markets were held in the old days and many thousands of head were exchanged.

Most of Skye's local inns brought tents on market days so that they could cash in on a share of the money that changed hands. At the close of trading, the drovers and their fine cattle-dogs would set off on the long journey south to the trysts of Falkirk and Crieff. One local drover, known as *Am Buideal*, the keg (not in any alcohol context, but because of his body shape), although illiterate, was said to recognise all the animals he had purchased and the price he had paid for each, although he dealt in hundreds. To this day, *Sluggans* is the venue for our cattle and sheep sales.

Until very recently the peat moss was used as the *Lagois Mhòr* or Big Midden, where all of the island's waste was consigned to land-fill. *Lughdaich, Ath-chleachd 's Ath-chuartaich* (Reduce, Re-use and Re-cycle) are the buzzwords nowadays, so the waste now travels by large diesel-guzzling lorries to various parts of Scotland; we have re-cycling points around the island from where the large, bright and garish colour-coded containers tumble over in the high winds scattering refuse in all directions! One good thing that's come out of this is that the local seagulls have had to forage elsewhere, allowing the emergency helipad to operate without the fear of sucking herring gulls through the air-intakes!

Between *Achachork* and *Drumuie* once lay the now long-abandoned township of *Achtalean*. There are many such deserted villages in Skye, but this one is remembered as the birthplace of one of the island's most influential sons. Donald Munro was born here in 1773 becoming an excellent exponent of the highland fiddle. At the age of fourteen he contacted smallpox which left him blind. Munro was a popular entertainer and travelled a great deal around north Skye. On one occasion in 1805, at an open-air meeting in *Uig*, he came in contact with John Farquharson, an evangelist from Glen Tilt in Perthshire, whose ship, on passage to America, had become stormbound in the sheltered bay. Farquharson was described by Principal Daniel Dewar of Marischal College, Aberdeen as *"the most wonderful man I have ever known, Divine power accompanied his ministry."* It was surely this Divine power which led to the conversion of the blind fiddler who became the "Father of Evangelical Religion" in Skye, and, not without significance, that the text on which the preacher spoke was, *'I am the door; by me if any man enter in he shall be saved, and shall go in and out and find pasture'*, as the doors of the Established Church had been shut to the large gathering!

The doors of the National Church in several parts of Skye remained closed to Donald Munro and those who espoused his revivalist doctrine, but the ordinary people of Skye had an open heart for this popular preacher and, like his Lord and Master, it was said that *"the common people heard him gladly"*. He was led by the hand from place to place, and there were those even prepared to carry him on their backs if need be. Following the revival of 1812 to 1814, during which very large numbers of people, of all ages, were converted, it appears to have been universally acknowledged, even by the opposing clergy, that the effects on the island were extremely positive. In later years, many writers have commented disparagingly on Munro for having had an adverse effect on the traditional music of Skye, as he had burned his own fiddle when he found a greater joy, and encouraged others to do likewise.

Donald Munro is buried in the old St. Columba graveyard on the island in the *Snizort* River, also, in the same grave, are the remains of his friend and fellow evangelist, Murdo MacDonald, a weaver from Stornoway. Murdo's last journey was to Skye to visit Blind Donald and they had sweet fellowship together. Murdo, however, took ill and became concerned that he would not be able to return to his native island. A few days before he died he became concerned as to the place of his burial. *"You shall rest in my own lair and we shall rise together"*, was Donald's assurance.

The main road, now the A87, does not go through the township of *Drumuie* but the construction engineer chose to take it over the hill, *Druimuidhe* (the yellow ridge, or perhaps, the ridge of the level country), between that village and *Borve*. No problem for travellers nowadays, but it is recorded that passengers on the stagecoaches of the late 19th Century were annoyed when they were forced to alight and walk up the hill to relieve the load on the horses. On one occasion, Joseph Chamberlain, then President of the Board of Trade, and one of the most important politicians of the century, father of Prime Minister Neville Chamberlain, observed this "problem" for himself as he travelled from *Kilmuir* to *Portree*.

The interest of politicians of all shades in the Highland Question had been raised by the events connected with the forced emigrations of the 19th Century and the pressing need for famine relief.

Another southern visitor to this part of the World was Alexander Smith who wrote the wonderfully romantic diary '*A Summer in Skye*'. Smith's father-in-law was Charles MacDonald of *Ord*, whom he refers to as Mr M'Ian. Although its title suggests that he had made only one summer visit, it is known that the book is compiled from his annual holidays here which began with his marriage in 1857 to Flora MacDonald, a blood-relative of the famous heroine. From this year until 1864 he continued his love-affair with Skye.

Writing of his drive by dog-cart from *Portree* to *Dunvegan*, Smith says, *"About three miles out of Portree I came upon a solitary-looking school-house by the wayside and a few yards further on a division of roads. A finger-post informed me that the road to the right led to Uig, that to the left to Dunvegan"*. This junction is of course at *Borve* and the little school-house was very likely the original MacDiarmid School.

In 1835, a certain Donald MacDiarmid, a native of *Borve*, died in Charleston, South Carolina. Along with his will, which granted various goods, chattels and money to relatives, and a Negro slave, named Clarissa, to a certain Jane Nicolson and family, there was an interesting letter to be forwarded to Lord MacDonald's Factor.

"Providence has, in his dispensation, directed my steps to this country and, here, blessed my labours, so far as to enable me to bestow some benefit on some others of my fellow creatures, and I know of no part of the world where its inhabitants should be benefited by me with more propriety than that of my nativity, and, as I have witnessed and am well aware of the disadvantages, of those who are illiterate labour under, particularly when thrown among people of different manners and customs from their own, I think I can in no way dispose of my effects better than to establish an English school for the education of the poor children of my native parish, and I have therefore deposited in the hands of Mr Macdonald £1,025 stg."

"The Rev Coll Macdonald of Portree, the two other ministers, the Factor of Trotternish, and Mr Macdonald of Kingsburgh, are to act as trustees. The money is to be invested and the income to be used to provide a permanent rent fund for the support of the school. Ground is to be leased to the trustees for a site on which to build it."

A suitable piece of land was leased on the farm of *'Peincharrain in the district of Borve'*, at Whitsun 1835. *"In building a schoolhouse and improving an acre of land for the schoolmaster, about £200 were expended by the trustees, which lessened considerably the original fund; yet by accumulation of interest and good management they expect to give a salary of £35 to the schoolmaster who is allowed to take moderate fees from such scholars as can afford them. The school is in high repute and numerously attended."*

We understand that the first headmaster was a Hugh Budge of *Kilmuir*. Mr Budge retired in 1891.

In his *Old Skye Tales*, William MacKenzie tells us that this first MacDiarmid School was closed at about this time, due to insufficient pupils in the *Borve* area, no doubt as a result of clearance, and the trust fund transferred to the present MacDiarmid School, built at *Carbost* in 1893. The first headmaster here was Mr MacIver, a Lewisman.

These days, *Borve* is a vibrant locality and was recently chosen as a Monitor Township by the Scottish Agricultural Colleges to provide examples of ways forward for Crofting Communities, but we fear that the actions of successive Governments, both at Westminster and Holyrood, but particularly Brussels, have not encouraged those with a genuine interest in keeping the land in good heart. Why are we content to accept poorer quality food from abroad when we can grow and nurture the purest, healthiest produce from highland hills and lochs? Perhaps in a day and age when it is he who shouts loudest that alone is heard, we are still too reticent. But long may we remain free from the brashness that characterises many from the south.

In 1993, when the estate came up for sale, in order to protect their rights, *Borve* and *Annishader* Township Limited was formed. With help from the Scottish Land Fund, they were able to purchase 4,502 acres. This particular buy-out was unique in that it was the first in Scotland to consider opening it to all of the estate's residents - not just the crofters.

Since the 1886 Crofters' Act, tenants in the Crofting Counties have had security of tenure and can no longer be forcibly evicted and sent to the Carolinas or Prince Edward Island at the whim of a landlord. Since 1976, Crofters have had the right to purchase their land from the landlord but little advantage in doing so, other than to further sell off valuable agricultural plots for housing. Certainly, this may be a short-term gain for some, but is to the future disadvantage of the industry and lifestyle in general; like selling off the family silver!

Perhaps estate purchase is the way forward, to empower local people to make better use of the land, both for the benefit of humans and the other animal and plant residents in our environment.

Little thought was given to the residents, human or otherwise in the 19th century, when whole townships were cleared on the MacLeod and MacDonald Estates to make way for the lucrative cheviot sheep whose wool spun a fortune for their owners.

Just a little north of *Borve* is the easily accessible *Breasclan* township, once a thriving example of community, but now deserted ruins. To sit here a while, brings a lump to the throat as we contemplate man's inhumanity to man.

"Ach dh'fhalbh an t-àm sin 's tha
'n gleann fo bhròn;
Bha 'n tobht aig Anndra 's e làn de
fheanntaig
Toirt na mo chuimhne nuair bha
mi òg."

"That time has gone and the glen is
sorrowful;
The now nettle-filled ruins of
Andrew's home
Remind me of when I was young."

Many of the names of the other townships which made up the MacDonald Collective Farms on the *Snizort Estate* are long forgotten by local folk. They were:- *Peinduin, Pein-cnoc-erisco, Peincharrain, Peinahuilinn, Birchisco, Breachagh, Scorinis and Escadile.*

Dun Borve would have provided sanctuary and communications for the local population in Viking times. It is visible from *Dun Gerishader* near *Portree* and in line with *Duns Sgalair, Suladale* and *Cruinn* which could provide commanding views of any naval activity on Loch *Snizort*. Robin Murray often drew our attention to these important lookout points on the map of Skye.

West of *Borve*, a settlement called *Cnoc a' Crò* was created for travelling people, in the early 1900s. These true tinkers, mainly of Stewart extraction, journeyed around the Highlands and Islands exercising their trade as tinsmiths. Milking pails, pots and pans were sold and repaired, usually for payment in kind. They lived in their traditional tents of tarpaulin stretched over hoops of willow or hazel, but were warm and comfortable due to the wood-burning stoves on which they prepared their meals. Only nowadays, through the broadcasts of Jessie Kesson and the writings of Betsy Whyte and Jess Smith, are we beginning to appreciate the vast knowledge of their natural surroundings that these people accumulated. They lived close to nature, were alive to weather patterns and were keen observers of the behaviour of birds and animals. Skilled horse breeders, they were always to the fore at the autumn sales which often took place at crossroads such as *Borve*. Traditionally, it was here that the Highland cattle from *Trotternish* joined the herds from the Western Isles which were landed at *Dunvegan*. Along with *Borve*, *Sligachan* and *Broadford* were the trysting points where the drovers augmented their herds.

By 1951 the travelling people had been re-settled in corrugated iron dwellings nearer to *Skeabost* where the concrete foundations of their houses may still be seen.

Alexander Smith talks of the discomfort of the 'Skye hut', as he calls the native, thatched 'blackhouse' of the time. *"During my wanderings I had the opportunity of visiting several of these dwellings and seeing how matters were transacted within. Frankly speaking, the Highland hut is not a model edifice. It is open to wind and always pervious to rain. An old bottomless herring firkin stuck in the roof usually serves for a chimney, but the blue peat-reek disdains that aperture and steams wilfully through the door and the crannies in the walls and roof. The interior is seldom well lighted – what light there is proceeding rather from the orange glow of the peat-fire, on which a large pot is simmering, than from the narrow pane with its great bottlegreen bull's-eye. The rafters which support the roof are black and glossy with soot, as can be seen by the sudden flashes of firelight. The sleeping accommodation is limited and the beds are composed of heather or fearns. The floor is the beaten earth, the furniture scanty; there is hardly ever a chair – stools and stones, worn smooth by the usage of several generations, have to do instead."*

"One portion of the hut is not unfrequently a byre and the breath of the cow is mixed with the odour of peat-reek and the baa of the calf mingles with the wranglings and swift ejaculations of the infant Highlanders. In such a hut as this there are sometimes three generations."

In the Autumn of 1841, Lord Cockburn, a Scottish circuit judge, having witnessed the impoverished local people dressed immaculately for a church service, was moved to say: *"I cannot comprehend how such purity can come out of such smoky hovels."*

In this same period, Sheriff Nicolson was writing of these same inhabitants, his relatives and friends.

"Reared in those dwellings have brave ones been;
brave ones are still there.
Forth from their darkness on Sunday I've seen
coming pure linen,
and, like the linen, the souls were clean
of them that wore it.

See that thou kindly use them, O man;
to whom God giveth
stewardship over them in thy short span,
not for thy pleasure!
Woe be to them who choose for a clan
four-feeted people!"

From *Glengrasco* a stream flows down by *Garalapin* and *Carbost* to join the *Skeabost* River. During the 18th Century, Skye, and its large population, became fertile ground for travelling merchants or packmen, many of whom were Irish. One such pedlar sought shelter for the night from an old couple along the way. In spite of the poverty suffered, Highland hospitality is well known and praised throughout the country and, true to form, the good people made him welcome. After a hearty meal they all retired to rest, the couple in their box bed and the guest in the *clòsaid* (closet). Although the exterior walls of 'blackhouses' were very thick, the same could not be said of the internal partitions. The packman overheard the *cailleach* say; "It's time to slaughter the wedder-goat (*eibhrionnach*)." "I'll do it in the morning", was the reply from the *bodach*." Now the Gaelic for Irishman is *Eireannach* which sounds much the same as *eibhrionnach*. In mortal fear, the pedlar ran from the house and, stumbling into the swollen burn in the dark, was drowned. Hence the name of the stream is *Lòn an Eireannaich*, the Irishman's burn.

This burn flows by the present MacDairmid School in the township of *Carbost* where we rejoin the '*Great North Road*'.

CHAPTER 3
South Snizort
Skeabost to Lynedale

The *River Snizort* is the longest and one of the principal salmon rivers of Skye. Its tributaries rise in *Glenmor* and *Glen Tungadal* and join the main outflow of *Loch Dubhagriach* at *Achaleathan*. Swift flowing, as it tumbles down through *Peiness,* it widens, slows and meanders by *Skeabost* Farm, forming ox-bow lakes and islands. These flat pasture lands make excellent pitches for shinty and football. One such field was known as the '*bugha mór*' and was often the venue for tussles with the *caman,* as the shinty stick is known. *Màiri Mhòr* remembered with affection these great social occasions from her youth, when the communities of *Skeabost* and *Bernisdale* would gather to watch the young men demonstrate their *camanachd* skills.

"Le buideal air gach ceann dhe'n raon,

agus pailteas bhonnach agus caise...."

"With a keg at each end of the field and
plenty of bannocks and cheese..."

It was traditional to play these games at the New Year or Old New Year (12th January, which was celebrated throughout the Highlands and Islands well into the 20th Century).

It was here, near *Skeabost* (sheltered farm), that *Màiri Mhòr* was born in 1821, the daughter of Iain Macdonald, *Iain Bàn Mac Aonghais Oig.* In her young days she was known as *Màiri*

Nighean Iain Bhàin (Mairi daughter of fair-haired Iain). A little to the south of the present cemetery, on the track which links the fields of *Skeabost* Farm, 'The Roman Road', is *Tobar Iain* Bhàin (Iain Ban's well), so the family home must have been close to this spot. What a wonderful view we get from here and, on a beautiful spring day, it is easy to imagine that this was the cradle of her inspiration and the picture in her mind's eye as she composed *Soraidh le Eilean a' Cheo* (Farewell to the Isle of Skye).

"Soraidh leis an àit'	"Farewell to the place
An d'fhuair mi m'àrach òg,	Where I was brought up
Eilean nam beann àrda	Island of high mountains
Far an tàmh an ceò;	Where the mist dwells;
Air am moch a dh'èireas	On which the sun rises early
Grian nan speur fo ròs,	Rosy in the heavens,
A'fuadach neul na h-oidhche,	Chasing away the shadows of night
Soillseachadh an Stòrr."	And illuminates the Storr."

As she wrote this poem, the former holdings were empty and the people had gone. How uplifting it is now to look out across *Carbost, Crepikill, Peinmore* and *Tote* and to see new houses and young folk growing up! How it would have gladdened her heart!

Was it perhaps at *Tote* that St Columba slew the wild boar? A rock with a prominent 'hoofmark' is pointed out as the place where the wild creature's charge was brought to a halt when the good man prayed!

A few hundred metres northwest of *Tobar Iain* Bhàin is *Caroline Hill*. Most authorities have suggested that it was named after his former home by a Captain MacDonald who returned from the Carolinas after the American War of Independence but Major John MacDonald, late of *Tote*, had another tale to tell. He believed that the story was, in fact, the other way round and that the two American States were named after this hill! In 1770 Clan MacDonald purchased 100,000 acres of land on the eastern seaboard of what is now the USA and many Skye clansmen settled there, among them a contingent from *Skeabost*. The Major believed that the Carolinas were thus named from their homeland. As evidence, he could produce a fairly recent letter from the authorities in North Carolina, asking him, as landowner, to allow a change of name for *Caroline Hill* to *Carolina Hill* to help cement the relationship with the home country. Typically, his reply to them was that, as they were the newcomers, they should be the ones to correct their address!

No stone now remains of *Caroline House* which was latterly the home of Otta Swire's grandmother's Aunt Jessie, who moved there after her brother, Kenneth MacLeod of *Greshornish (Coinneach Mòr Gheusto)* died in 1869. In her excellent book *'Skye: The Island and its Legends'*, Swire gives a lovely picture of the homeliness of this cottage and tells of the vast store of folk-tales, legends and facts that Miss Jessie had at her fingertips.

On crossing the *Snizort* River we come into MacLeod Country (*Dùthaich Mhic Leòid*), as the river formed the boundary between MacDonald and MacLeod territory from 1539. *Skeabost* was the scene of at least two clan battles between these, the largest of Skye's clans. The present Golf Course, belonging to the *Skeabost* Country House Hotel, is situated on *Buaile Bhlair*, the Battle Ground, and *Achadh na Fala*, the Field of Blood, and there is a commemorative cairn on the east side of the river below Tote. Nowadays, thankfully, no blood flows on the Golf Course but blood sports continue as wild sea-trout and salmon are still caught in the deep pools of the river.

The former *Skeabost* Post Office was an important one and originally a coaching inn known as *Tigh a Ribaigh (meaning unknown)*. Major McGuffie late of Skeabost Farm maintained that it was the oldest in Skye but *Stein* and *Edinbane* also make this claim.

When Skeabost House was in building, an apprentice would be sent down the drive to the inn, to bring a bucket of ale to the thirsty workforce. The Post Office was particularly important as this was a true crossroads. The mail coaches from *Bracadale* came down by the 'Roman Road' and the old road continued north from here via *Prabost* to *Uig*, crossing the *Portree /Dunvegan* road at *Skeabost*.

I remember the remnants of a superb, one and a half mile long, beech hedge which still bounded the policies of Skeabost House in my young days. J. A. MacCulloch in 1905 waxed lyrical in his description of it; *"Appearing suddenly after the naked landscape and the waste moor strewn with boulders, it looks as if a bit of England had been transferred to these moorland solitudes. So accurately is it cut that it undulates and winds with every winding and dip of the road, suggesting a pair of long sinuous green serpents, like the monsters of the romantic Celtic folk-tales. In winter it keeps its russet-brown leaves when all the trees around are bare, and as it catches the hues of the fiery winter sunsets it blazes like burnished bronze. In spring the change from brown to green is gradual. First one notes the light greenish-white tint dawning amid the russet; then the mingling of green and brown; the fading of the brown as the old leaves fall off, until the long winding road is encompassed with walls of emerald."*

As we pass by these days, we notice that the beeches now form rows of fully grown mature trees at some distance from the present road.

It was Lachlan MacDonald, a nephew of Miss Jessie, who built and adorned the present *Skeabost* House in the latter half of the 19th Century. The marriage of Lachlan's parents had linked the family of Gesto MacLeods with the MacDonalds of *Kingsburgh*, Flora MacDonald's descendants. 'As rich as *Skeabost*' became a proverb in Skye! It is interesting, as already mentioned, that one of Lachlan's nieces, also Flora, married Alexander Smith, author of '*A Summer in Skye*'.

Lachlan, the seventh landlord of *Skeabost* since MacLeod of MacLeod sold the estate, had succeeded John Robertson and, after a bad start, taking seven crofters to court in 1872 to prevent them gathering shellfish from Loch *Snizort*, he soon had a change of heart. We are told that his whole attitude to his tenantry softened when he came under the influence of the Gospel (*"thàinig atharrachadh nan gràs air"*). He soon set about ameliorating the lot of his tenants. Unlike many of the landlords of the time, he helped by providing employment, in making roads, in improvements to the estate and in transforming the house into a beautiful mansion. While other crofters fought for fair rents, Lachlan asked his tenants themselves to fix the rent for each holding. This seems to have been done to the satisfaction of both sides. This enlightenment was apparently extended to the cottars, or landless people, living on the estate. He gave them plots of land and helped defray the cost of housing. On several occasions he helped the poor by supplying them with seed potatoes and oats. He was regarded as very approachable, and as his language was their language, he was able to deal with their complaints and requests at first hand.

He it was who gave Woodside Cottage, rent free, to Màiri Mhòr and paid for the first publication of her songs in 1891. All her poetry was written down at her prompting by John White, as she could not write. What a wonderful memory she must have had!

Col. Kenneth MacDonald DSO of *Tote* was one of Lachlan's six sons and his heir. He commanded the Lovat Scouts with distinction in the Boer War, Macedonia and at the Dardanelles. Many Skyemen served under the command of this popular soldier and it is said that he continued to take a great interest in the families of those to whom he had become so attached. Kenneth was forced to sell the *Skeabost* Estate to pay for the bond that supported the *Gesto* Hospital.

In 1921, the *Skeabost* Estate reverted again to the hands of Clan MacLeod when it was purchased from the MacDonalds by

Duncan MacLeod. Duncan was one of eleven children from a *Broadford* crofting family, who is reputed to have left Skye with a half-crown in his pocket and returned a millionaire in the days when millionaires were few and far between. As an export manager for a firm in Glasgow, he built up contacts around the world. He managed the whisky firm of Bulloch Lade which he then sold to the Distillers Co Ltd and set up the firm of Duncan MacLeod and Co which had an annual turnover of £15m in its heyday. He was a philanthropist who took an interest in Highland affairs, particularly Shinty. In 1926, he presented the *Skeabost* Horn Trophy (a replica of Rory Mòr's Drinking Horn) for annual competition by the league clubs in the South of Scotland. The Glasgow Skye Association and An Comunn Gaidhealach also benefited from his interest. While a student at Glasgow University, I was fortunate to get a very welcome annual grant from his competitive education fund.

Duncan was an associate of Donald Cumming who owned *Glenvaragill* Farm near *Portree* and *Borlum* Farm at *Drumnadrochit,* and who has given his name to the Cummings Hotel, Inverness.

We are told that these two very rich Skyemen, involved in the Hotel trade and whisky industry, attracted the attention of certain American gentlemen during Prohibition times. Over the years, *Skeabost* House has had many famous and distinguished guests, including Sir Harry Lauder, but perhaps none as well known as Al Capone! He is said to have stayed there and 'shot some pool' on the snooker table! What was discussed we must leave to the reader's imagination ...

In his book, *'Over the Sea to Skye'*, Alasdair Alpin MacGregor tells us that; *"long was Loch Snizort a lurking place for smugglers"*. From the files of the *Inverness Courier* we see that in 1829 a large smuggling lugger was captured in Loch *Snizort* with a crew of eleven and a valuable cargo of gin, tea, tobacco and snuff. Long before that, in 1744 at a magistrates' meeting in Portree, the gentlemen present bound themselves not to drink smuggled tea, and to do all in their power, *"if it is humanly possible,"* to prevent their wives and daughters from doing so!

In Alexander Nicolson's *'History of Skye'* he tells us that *"the import of wines from France and Spain began about the middle of the sixteenth century but until its last decade the people of Skye were fairly temperate. Soon, however, the love of strong drink, imported brandy and native whisky, was to seize gentle and simple alike, and great excesses were the result."* In the 'Regulations for Chiefs', issued by the Government in 1616, the consumption of alcohol was blamed for the, *"beastly and barbarous cruelties and inhumanities that fall out among them to the offence and the displeasure of God and the contempt of law and justice."*

At the funeral of the chief of Clan Donald, Sir Alexander, who died in 1746 and was buried at Kilmore in Sleat, *"£2,645* (an enormous sum in those days) *was spent, and drink was dispensed with such a lavish hand that acts of riotous revelry ensued. In the fights that took place, many were grievously injured."*

It is, therefore, quite remarkable that by the mid 1800s the people of Skye were again being described, by their ministers, as temperate. In 1841, Rev A Clark of Duirinish wrote; *"The people are generally remarkably sober. Their hospitality continues as unbounded as ever; but in their exercise of it the rules of temperance and decorum are very rarely violated, and every excess is condemned and discouraged".* Rev Coll MacDonald of Portree says; *"such vices as profane swearing and drunkenness are less prevalent than they were twenty years ago. The people are powerfully under the influence of moral principles, so much so that heinous crimes are seldom or ever seen or heard among them".*

It was in 1830 that the first legal distillery was constructed at Carbost in Minginish (now the famous Talisker distillery). The Rev Roderick MacLeod, then minister at Bracadale describes it as, *"one of the greatest curses that, in the ordinary course of providence, could befall this or any other place."*

Our journey continues from *Skeabost*, over the River *Tora* to *Bernisdale*.

By the shore of Loch *Snizort Beag*, at *Inver Tora*, are the large Church and Manse of the Free Church built for *Maighstir Ruaraidh,* but the corrugated iron Church of Scotland, that I remember from my youth, has gone.

Land for a home and meeting house was granted here, at *Pairc a' Fhraoich,* to Blind Donald Munro by 'The Lady of Kingsburgh's family' in 1817. Later, the Rev Roderick MacLeod's wife, Annie, who was the daughter of the Skeabost landowner, and had been virtually disowned when her husband left the Established Church, returned home to beg a piece of land from her father on which to build a Free Church, as huge numbers of people continued to meet here in all weathers for divine service. He replied that he had known that she would one day come begging. Her spirited reply, to the effect that she was not begging for herself but for her father's tenants, must have melted his heart. He asked for how long she wished the lease. *"For a thousand years and a day"* was her repost. It was this same lady, on hearing that her husband had been ejected from his church at *Kensaleyre*, said, *"I would rather have news of his death than that he had gone back on his principles".*

It is worthy of note that the Rev Angus Martin, who replaced Roderick as minister in the Established Church in the parish, was his childhood friend and this friendship continued until Roderick's death.

By the side of the Free Church is another imposing white-washed building, which was once a school, but is now the Church Hall. Mary Ann MacFarlane, a member of the local Community Council since its inception 33 years ago, tells me that her grandfather was the caretaker here and that his family lived on the upper floor. It was in this area that Màiri Mhòr lived at Woodside Cottage *("Bothan Ceann na Coille")* after her return to Skye, having qualified as a nurse in Glasgow. It says much for her determination that she was in her 50s before embarking on her nursing studies.

She was much in demand as a midwife and delivered Mary Ann's aunt Marion Shaw. The new mother was horrified when

Mairi asked that a bath be filled with water from the river and the baby dipped in the cold water. It didn't do the child any harm. She was third of a family of eight and outlived all the other family members. Indeed, throughout her life she was noted for never having felt the cold! Perhaps the early bath was indeed beneficial!

Here at the mouths of the *Snizort* and *Tora*, when I was young, salmon and sea trout were quietly poached under cover of the gloaming which passes for night in a Skye summer. This practice, although wrong in the eyes of the law, was looked on as acceptable by many families, who still regard deer on the hill and fish in the water as belonging to **all** mankind.

Adult wild Atlantic salmon return to the freshwater streams in which they were hatched after spending time feeding in the waters between Iceland and Greenland. Grilse, having spent one year at sea, return to home waters from July onwards and make a very tasty meal. But times are changing. Numbers of wild salmon have fallen considerably in recent years due to several factors including disease, over fishing and possible inter-breeding with escapees from the many salmon farms which are now to be found around our coasts. Work on these farms has been very welcome in Skye but automation means that they are no longer as labour intensive as they were in the early days of the industry and the work can disappear as quickly as it arrived. The little crofter-enterprise fish farms, which promised so much, are almost all gone and the Norwegians have the lion's share. Vikings back to their old games!

The proprietors of the *Skeabost* Estate would regularly net the mouth of the *Snizort* River, often taking more than 100 salmon on a flood tide. John Robertson, owner before Lachlan MacDonald, was also fisheries officer in the 1850s and 60s. At that time, of course, herring was the most important species. As well as catching them by netting, the use of Karries *(Cairidh)* became important. These were fish-traps built with stone between low and high tide. There was a famous one in Loch

Snizort which was more than a quarter of a mile long. It was free for all the community to take fish from the *Cairidh*, as the tide retreated, except for a 'pocket in the bend' reserved for the tacksman. Derek Cooper in his book "Skye" tells us that salmon were caught in this way from May to August and then the herring shoals would come into the loch from September to November. Sometimes as many as 50 to 60 cran of herring could be taken on a tide! A cran was equal to four boxes!

Fresh herring, now a luxury, were fried in oatmeal and eaten with potatoes but the bulk of the catch would be salted in barrels for the winter. It is now almost impossible to get a decent salt herring although salt mackerel are making a comeback. As I grew up, we always had a keg of salt herring and a bag of Kerr's Pink or Golden Wonder potatoes on standby.

From Victorian times, most of the *Cairidhs* in Skye's sea lochs were broken up by the landowners who wanted the game fish for their tenants, who were prepared to pay large sums for the summer rental of the 'sporting estates'. A Skyeman writing in 1930 of the *Snizort Cairidh* said: *"It was broken down and today not a trace of it is seen, inevitable through progressive encroachments on sea and land by the privileged class."*

Cooper's entry in his gazetteer in this connection is worth quoting.

"Around the middle of the nineteenth century a new industry hit the Highlands and spilled over into the Islands. Large fat men from the Midlands paid even larger and fatter sums of money to be allowed to slaughter anything which could be coaxed and beaten within gun range." By 1885, the shooting rents for some Skye estates were netting more than £1000 per year for the proprietors.

These forays of *"the privileged class"* into the Highlands during Victorian times, was to become the beginning of Skye's Tourist Industry which is now, by far, the island's largest source of income.

The Jetty at *Skeabost* House was the delivery point for the local coal club. Puffers brought this fuel for the community in the first half of the 20th century. It was also one of the many emigration points from which the people said a sad farewell as they embarked for the American Continent.

Bernisdale (Bjorn's dale) is another reminder of the Norse influence in this part of Skye. All around the 12 mile length of Loch *Snizort* are names of Viking origin.

There are four distinctive townships in *Bernisdale, Glen, Mains, Park* and *Aird*, all of which have their share of the affluent properties which have become common on Skye. This affluence does not come from the fact that these are crofting communities, as for many, this is the loss-making part of their business, but that they have diversified to cater for the much more lucrative B&B and Self-catering trade. The outstanding beauty of this island, and its romantic connotations, encourage visitors from all around the world. Those few who are disappointed by a spell of poor weather have an added incentive to come again!

Our journey continues by the woods of *Treaslane*, believed to have been planted around the policies of *Treaslane* House by John Martin for whom the Dr John Martin Memorial Hospital at *Uig* has been named. He was one from the famous family of Martins of *Marishadder* who were referred to in *'Like a Bird on the Wing'*. After John Martin's death, *Treaslane* House became the property of Alexander MacDonald, Lord MacDonald's Factor at the time of the Land Agitation.

It was here that Alexander Smith observed *"two bare-footed and bare-headed girls yoked to a harrow and dragging it up and down a small plot of delved ground."* This incident prompted him to compare the lives of the native Skye peasants with city dwellers of his day. His descriptions and conclusions paint a lively picture of the social conditions of the poor in the mid 19th century.

Having described the inadequacies of the 'black house' he turns his attention to the positive side.

"Am I inclined to lift my hands in horror at witnessing such a dwelling? Certainly not. I have only given one side of the picture. The home I speak of nestles beneath a rock, on the top of which dances the ash-tree and the birch. The emerald mosses on its roof are softer and richer than the velvets of kings. Twenty yards down that path is a well that needs no ice in the dog-days. At a little distance, from rocky shelf to rocky shelf, trips a mountain burn, with abundance of trout in the brown pools. At the distance of a mile is the sea, which is not allowed to ebb and flow in vain; for in the smoke of the house there is a row of fishes drying; and on the floor a curly-headed urchin of three years or thereby is pummelling the terrier with the scarlet claw of a lobster. Methought, too when I entered I saw beside the door a heap of oyster shells.

Depend upon it there are worse odours than peat-smoke, worse neighbours than a cow or a brood of poultry; and although a couple of girls dragging a harrow be hardly in accordance with our modern notions, yet we need not forget that there are worse employments for girls than even that."

Describing the consequences of not having money for a horse, the representative from *Glen Bernisdale*, when addressing the *Napier Commission*, was much more concerned. He said, *"We must make a horse's work out of a woman, we get them to harrow – while slavery is done away with in other countries it is likely to continue here!"*

Clachamish and *Suladale* are the next two townships we pass and, from the headland at *Knott*, we get a superb view of the Western Isles as Loch *Snizort* widens out to provide our picture frame. This point is *Rudha nan Cudaigean*. Most sea lochs in Skye have their Cuddy Point from which, during September to November, we can fish for plentiful young whiting or coalfish. In our area we used a long cane rod with baited hooks. Small the cuddies may be but how sweet! Straight from the sea to the frying-pan! A feast!

The well known Skye band *Runrig* sing of *Rudha nan Cudaigean*. I had thought they had based the song on the Cuddy Point in Portree Bay but the words refer to a different method of cuddy fishing which is still used in parts of Skye but is more common in Harris and Lewis. A large circular net called the *tàmh* is used, baited with softened limpets. The song is in the traditional style composed for daily work tasks such as fishing, rowing, milking, herding and harvesting.

	4 actions
Buainidh sinn na bàirnich, na bàirnich, na bàirnich,	Gather the limpets, the limpets, the limpets,
Goilidh sinn na bàirnich, na bàirnich, na bàirnich,	Boil the limpets, the limpets, the limpets,
Cagnaidh sinn na bàirnich, na bàirnich, na bàirnich,	Chew the limpets, the limpets, the limpets,
Sgaoilidh sinn na bàirnich na bàirnich, na bàirnich.	Scatter the limpets, the limpets, the limpets,
Nach ith sibh na bàirnich is ithidh mi na cudaigean.	Come and eat the limpets and I will eat the cuddies.

Dr Johnson said, *"The cuddy is a fish of which I know not the philosophical name. It is not much bigger than a gudgeon, but is of great use in these islands, as it affords the lower people both food and oil for their lamps. Cuddies are so abundant, at some times of the year that they are caught like whitebait in the Thames, only by dipping a basket and drawing it back."*

Tayinloan *(Tigh an Lòin)* was a busy inn when the stagecoach ran from *Portree* to *Dunvegan* and *Stein*. Also, at that time, it was where the herring fishermen took refreshment between setting and hauling their nets in Loch *Snizort*. Now it is a private house and the main road no longer passes the front door. In my youth, it was the home of Mr Ian Hilleary, Chairman of the County Council Roads Department, and painted a hideous pink! The gardens were always attractive, especially the lovely flowers which grew out of hollows on the bridge parapet. I often fished for trout in the stream, over which we had to cross to get to my Aunty Katie's house. This is now the immaculately kept diversified croft of Kenny and Charlotte Nicolson. Aunt Katie, like so many girls who remained in Skye, became a maid at 'the big houses' of the aristocracy. She worked at *Viewfield* and *Redcliff* and married the chauffeur, Donald MacKinnon.

Lynedale with its curiously shaped gatehouse is another of those farms/estates which benefited from the fashion for tree-planting which took hold in the early 1800s. Otta Swire mentions that *Lynedale, Orbost, Greshornish, Dunvegan* and *Gesto* woodlands all date from this period, the work of Alexander MacDonald of Balranald, and that the gardens of these fine houses were all the recipients of snowdrop bulbs brought back from the Crimea by Skyemen who fought in the war of that name. Certainly in February, the lovely carpets of snowdrops along the road to the *Lynedale* farmhouse are as she describes. Another description which we have heard is also very true: *"the woods of Lynedale are musical with birds"*.

On completion of his college course in Aberdeen, Roderick MacLeod, *Maighstir Ruaraidh,* was licensed to preach and was appointed to the mission of *Lynedale* in his father's parish.

The 3rd Lord Napier of Magdala, lived here for a short time in the early 1900s and improved the gardens. He imported soil from England, but inadvertently introduced moles which hitherto were not native to Skye. His grandfather, the 1st Lord Napier, Fellow of the Royal Society of London, with a special interest in Natural History, was *'the bughunter'* in George MacDonald Fraser's *'Flashman on the March'*. He rose to be a prominent soldier, Governor of Gibraltar and Commander of the British Army in India. In fact there is another Skye connection. He was deputy to the 8th Earl of Elgin, Viceroy of India, and took over these duties for a short time on Lord Elgin's death. This Earl of Elgin was the grandfather of the one for whom the Elgin Hostel is named. He was also the son of the Lord Elgin who "stole" the Elgin Marbles from Greece.

Lord Napier had purchased *Lynedale* from the family of another Alexander MacDonald who had made his name in the construction industry. This gentleman, like so many before and since, had to leave Skye to seek employment in the south. With diligence and application, he worked his way upwards until he was managing some of the most important civil engineering projects in Scotland. He built several bridges throughout the country and employed Skyemen whenever possible. Many spoke highly of his consideration and treatment of his employees. His firm helped to build the Highland Railway from Dingwall to the west. In particular, he took charge of the section between *Strome Ferry* and *Kyle of Lochalsh* and blasted through the solid rock at *Creag Dallaig*. This stretch was once called *'the most expensive 12 miles of railway in the world'*. It is now recognised as one of the most enchanting!

Many of the contracts he took on had a penalty clause in case of late completion. He often finished them ahead of time! On one bridge project he charged a toll between the date of completion and the contracted finishing date to net his firm a large profit. In Skye itself, MacDonald contracted to build this next part of the 'Great North Road' between *Snizort* and *Dunvegan* which he completed in 1811.

"'S mi gun coisicheadh le sunnd
An rathad ùr triomh thìr MhicLeòid."

"I would traverse with cheer
The new road through MacLeod country."

Alexander also made a contribution to the defence of the island. In 1803 it was decided to raise two regiments locally when fear of France was at its height throughout Britain. James MacLeod, Chief of Raasay, commanded one regiment and Alexander of *Lynedale* the other. They were each given rank of lieutenant-colonel. After Trafalgar, confidence returned to the country, and Skye's Home Defence regiments were disbanded.

Lynedale Farm was the first to use the revolutionary 'swing plough' which Alexander brought to the island in 1791. It was said to have revolutionised farming on the island.

Not surprisingly, Màiri Mhòr penned some verses in praise of this industrious Skyeman.

"Is iomadh iad tha seinn do chliù,
Le dùrachd mar a b'fhiach dhaibh,
'S ann chuir thu onair air do dhùthaich,

H-uile taobh na thriall thu;
Ni creagan Atadail a dhearbhadh,
Nach teid d'ainm air dhiochuimhn,

Fhad 's bhios tonnan uaine a'chuain,
Dol sios as suas mu Liandial".

Many are who sing your praise,
With goodwill as they ought to.
You have brought honour to your
district,
Everywhere you went.
The rocks of Attadale prove,
That your name will not be
forgotten,
As long as the green ocean waves,
Ebb and flow at Lynedale.

CHAPTER 4

From Skye Linen to Fairy Silk

Our journey continues from *Lynedale* (G. Flax valley), where linen was once woven, with *Braebost* (N. Broad Farm) to our left and *Fanks* (G. Flat fields enclosed by rocks) to the right, on towards *Flashadder* (G. Flat pasture land) and *Arnisort* (N. The Eagle's Loch). This positioning of townships with alternate Gaelic and Norse names is very typical in Skye. One imagines that, as the Vikings began to settle as farmers among the native Celts, there would be mutual suspicion between the communities. Only with time would they begin commercial activity, which in turn would lead to intermarriage and assimilation. Language differences would only gradually be overcome and the minority language would eventually lose out to the stronger. Do we observe the same scenario nowadays?

Kildonan (The church or cell of St. Donan) was once the parish church of Snizort but now, only the name remains as a reminder of the past. From here there are superb views to the Outer Hebrides and on rare occasions in late autumn and early spring, on clear frosty nights, free from the light pollution of cities and towns, a chance to view the *Fir Chlis* (Aurora Borealis, Northern Lights) or Heavenly Dancers. This phenomenon must have been particularly mysterious to our ancestors, perhaps as mind-boggling as the explanations that scientists now attempt! Be that as it may, the light show can by awe-inspiring, usually curtains of greens and blues with occasional pinks being drawn and redrawn across the sky.

Loch Greshornish with its fish and shellfish farms sparkles in the sunlight. This is a spectacularly beautiful and peaceful place but, on one occasion during World War I, its peace was shattered by the sound of explosions as a British seaplane attempted to flush out an enemy submarine which had taken refuge in the deep water. The mission was unsuccessful, but the incident had brought the War close to our shores for the first time. Few Skye families needed such reminders, as their sons and husbands were much more immediately involved!

Down by the loch-side beyond *Arnisort* is *Borve*. Yes, another one! Complete with its own *Dun Borve* – which is not surprising since the name *Borve* actually means a fort. This one is special according to Otta Swire, as it was reputed to have once been the home of a company of fairies who abandoned it suddenly when the local humans, finding them a bother, ganged up to shout; *"The fort is on fire! The fort is on fire!"* This frivolous use of the early 999 system ensured that this township, was never again, a happy one!

Fairies *(na daoine sìth)* were ubiquitous in Skye mythology. The females of the species were usually observed to wear green but the men were often attired in russet garments, dyed with *crotal*. Their usual abode was the *sìthean,* or green fairy knoll, into which unwary humans would be enticed by the sound of their music or the excitement of the fairy-dance. Belief in fairies, witches, the *evil-eye* and the *Gruagach* continued to the end of the 19th century and some, still living, claim to know someone who has/had *second-sight*. The *Gruagach* was believed to be a long-haired woman who controlled the yield of the flocks and herds. Her interference was usually malevolent unless conciliated by libations of milk poured, on Saturdays, into the hollow of the local *gruagach-stone*. In 1716 Martin Martin comments; *"there were scarce any, the least village in which this superstitious custom could not prevail. I enquired the reason for it from several well meaning people who, until of late had practised it, and they told me that it had been transmitted to them by their ancestors who believed it was attended with great fortune".* A local *Clach na Gruagaich* is pointed out at *Carbost, South Snizort.*

It is believed that these superstitions were not discouraged by St Columba and the other Celtic missionaries, who hoped that the superiority of the religion they preached would soon confine the ancient practices and beliefs to history.

Steeped in these beliefs, perhaps it is not surprising that the appearance of a mysterious creature in Loch *Greshornish,* one fine summer's day in the 1850s, nearly led to panic in the community. The visitor turned out to be a full-grown walrus, the only one ever known to have come to Skye; but, with global warming —- who knows!

In the 18th century, as the Highland Clan Chiefs began to spend more time with their aristocratic friends in the south, they sought new ways of acquiring cash to finance their lifestyle and gambling debts. One such way was to mortgage some of their land. The system of *wadset* was begun and soon many of the principal men of the clans paid money to the chiefs in return for the rental of an estate. *Wadsetters* became numerous in Skye in the 18th century and were virtually indistinguishable from *Tacksmen.* The MacLeods of *Gesto,* who could trace their lineage to Harold the Black, King of Iceland, latterly held their land in this way, although they had previously owned the *Gesto Estate* outright. In 1825, however, following a boundary dispute which *Gesto* won in court, they were vindictively evicted by John Norman the 24th Chief of Clan MacLeod. The last of the MacLeods of *Gesto* was Neil MacLeod, an expert on the history of the Highland Bagpipe. 'The Gesto Collection' of pipe music is justly renowned.

When Neil's son, Kenneth, retired from an active life as a tea and indigo planter, having amassed a fortune in India, he was disappointed to be refused the purchase or rental of the former family lands. Instead he bought the estates of *Greshornish,*

Orbost, Skeabost, Skirinish and Tote, but continued to be known as *Coinneach Mòr Gheusto* (Big Kenneth of Gesto).

As is usually quoted for Skyemen who have made good, Kenneth left for India *"with a golden guinea in his pocket and his fare paid"*, courtesy of Mrs MacDonald of Waternish. (He was luckier than Duncan MacLeod of Skeabost who set off *'with only a half-crown'*). After a year's work, Kenneth took the river boat down to Calcutta. On the way he went ashore and visited a place where an auction of the contents of a sugar factory was in progress. With his precious guinea, he bought a copper boiler, which he sold in Calcutta for £30. He then returned to the derelict sugar factory and bought it for very little. This set him on the ladder to riches. Personal contacts were an added bonus — he became a close friend of the Rajah of Hutival. His return to his homeland however, was tinged with sadness when his fiancé died in Paris.

Kenneth is *'The Landlord'* in Alexander Smith's book. In fact he was Smith's wife's uncle.

The author's description of his arrival at *Edinbane,* the *'small village established by the landlord'*, is an excellent piece of romantic writing although the *'facts'* are doubtless exaggerated.

"On the hillside, on my left as I drove (by dog-cart), stretched a long street of huts covered with smoky wreaths and in front of each a strip of cultivated ground ran down to the road which skirted the shore. Potatoes grew in one strip, turnips in a second, corn in a third and, as these crops were in different stages of advancement, the entire hillside, from the street of huts downward, resembled one of those counterpanes which thrifty housewives manufacture by sewing together the patches of different patterns.

"Along the road running at the back of the huts a cart was passing; on the moory hill behind, a flock of sheep, driven by men and dogs, was contracting and expanding itself like quicksilver. The women were knitting at the hut doors, the men were at work in the cultivated patches at front. On all this scene of cheerful and fortunate industry, on men and women, on turnips, oats and potatoes, on cottages set in azure films of peat-reek, the rosy light was striking – making a pretty spectacle enough. From the whole hillside breathed

peace, contentment, happiness and a certain sober beauty of usefulness. Men and nature seemed in perfect agreement and harmony – man willing to labour, nature to yield increase."

The village of *Edinbane (An t-Aodann Bàn,* the fair face*)*, unlike other townships in Skye, was indeed planned and settled so that each necessary trade was represented in the population. There was a mason, a joiner, a miller and a smith, as well as a school and merchant's shop, but no church. Smith tells us that *"divine service was held in the school-house on Sundays".*

The *Edinbane* Lodge Hotel claims to be the oldest coaching inn on Skye, dating from circa 1543. (This claim is also made by *Stein* Inn.) Rebuilt by Kenneth as a hunting lodge, it was the first place in Skye to have electricity, which came from a hydro scheme in the *Abhainn Choishleadar* behind the Lodge. The hotel is supposed to be haunted by various ghosts.

The *Edinbane* website tells us that; *"The Lodge was used as the district court for the surrounding area, where people were tried for sheep rustling and more serious crimes. If found guilty and sentenced to death, they were hanged in the gardens of the hotel!"* As the blurb does not tell us **when** this was the case, we are left with rather an uneasy feeling!

Kenneth's attempts at creating suitable 'holdings' for the poor cottars on '*Blackhill*' comes in for praise from Smith but, in spite of the rosy picture which he paints, these were hard times and the landlord, while encouraging industry among the people, was obliged to sell them meal and to make preparations for emigration.

Otta Swire tells us that Kenneth's *"emigration ship to Canada, had orders to remain there for some weeks so that it might bring back to Skye any who changed their minds or became homesick."*

If this was indeed the case, it was far from the norm, as mid 18th century landlords and conditions for an Atlantic crossing were usually such that few would wish to endure the return voyage!

Coinneach Mòr's lasting legacy was his endowment of the local hospital in 1869, the first in Skye and named *Gesto Hospital* after his birthplace. He guaranteed £800 per annum, his near neighbours Lachlan MacDonald of Skeabost £800 and MacDonald of Waternish £400, for the upkeep of the facility. For many years, not only was it important to Skye but also North Uist, as it provided the nearest operating theatre for that island, being a two hour voyage and one hour trap ride away! In 1948, the 12-bed hospital became part of the National Health Service and continued as a surgical unit until the late 1950s. During this time, care of some elderly folk became part of *Gesto's* duties. About once a month, specialists in ENT and Orthopaedics from Inverness held Health Clinics and performed operations on this site. By 1958 *Gesto* became identified as a long-stay geriatric unit and surgery was transferred to the MacKinnon Memorial Hospital in *Broadford*. In the early 1990s, local people had to fight a rearguard action to save it from the pen-pushers and accountants of the NHS who had earmarked it for closure in November 1991, following what passes for '*Consultation*'. I was present, along with six hundred others, in the *Marshall Centre in Edinbane*, to hear reasoned speeches in favour of retention of this facility. Reluctantly, the 'Powers That Be' backed down and the Hospital remained open until, by 2006, it had succumbed to the effects of neglect and lack of investment. An enthusiastic Steering Group now wish to purchase the boarded-up building for community use and have formed into a company limited by guarantee. Oh that public bodies would show some magnanimity when these facilities were gifted to them, for the good of the local community, all those years ago! Individual public servants must not hide behind bureaucracy and 'regulations' to deny the community the opportunity to allow the benefits of *Coinneach Mòr's* liberality to continue.

Much farther back in time, the tacksman of *Greshornish*, a certain Donald MacLeod, was recognised as an expert swordsman. He was chosen to give lessons to the young men at *Dunvegan Castle*. While demonstrating his skills, fencing with the heir, he proceeded to remove the buttons of his coat, one by one, with the point of his sword. The Chief called a halt to proceedings when the lad's collar stud flew off!

As I was growing up, the *Greshornish* Estate was owned by the *Portree* butcher, Donald Matheson. Like *Coinneach Mòr*, *Dòmhlan* was also a rich, self-made bachelor, but he had made his fortune at home in Skye. Trained as a teacher in Depression times, he taught Mathematics and Rural Studies in several Skye schools, (no way to make a fortune), before succeeding his father in the Wentworth Street firm of *M. Matheson, Butchers and Poulterers.*

As a teacher, Dolan's foibles were legendary. *"Watch the board while I go through it"* was the classic which he repeated regularly, to the amusement of the pupils, but as a stockman and butcher of local Skye produce he was unrivalled. His farm, on the *Greshornish* peninsula, produced quality beef and lamb for many years. Dolan's abattoir in *Portree* ensured that the journey from pasture to plate was a short one. Lack of proper slaughtering facilities in Skye, these days, is one of the biggest handicaps that the island crofters face. As usual, to absolve themselves of any blame, both Local and National Governments point the finger at the EU.

Our journey has now taken us through *Edinbane*, by *Coshletter* to the Red Burn, where the minor road to *Greshornish* Lodge and the famous Mussel Farms, leaves the main highway.

I found it interesting to discover that the rapidly growing woodland by the roadside is jointly owned by: *Karl Anselm Furst Von Urach Von Wurttemberg (Prinz Anselm)* and *Wilhelm Albert Furst Von Urach Graf Von Wurttemberg.*

I'm glad I've got a simple name. Ian makes life so much easier!

What's in a name? Well names are indeed important and each one of the ten Wind Turbines of the *Ben Aketil* Farm has got one, courtesy of young Donald Lockhart from *Struan* Primary School. In 2007, Donald was guest of honour at the opening ceremony for the first wind farm development on the island. He had won the naming competition organised by the Isle of Skye Renewables Co-operative. His choice of titles harks back to Viking times, as each turbine now has a name ending in *–bost* from the Norse *bolstadhr* meaning homestead, farm or steading. The names are:

Orbost, Eabost, Carbost, Colbost, Skeabost, Husabost, Heribost, Breabost, Prabost and *Kirkibost*.

The co-op was formed so that local people could own a stake in the farm and over 500 members were prepared to show their encouragement for the enterprise by investing between £250 and £20,000. The Dunvegan Community Trust also receives £32,000 per year from the profits, for the lifetime of the farm.

Ben Aketil produces enough electricity to power 17,000 homes! The present population of Skye is just over 10,000 individuals so we are self-sufficient in 'green energy'.

Like hydro, wind generation benefits the environment by replacing more polluting forms like coal, gas and oil and helps to fight against greenhouse gas emissions.

In my opinion, the turbines have been sited sensitively and do not detract from the visual magnificence of our island, although they can be seen from all the Wings of Skye. There are lots of places on the island where the visual impact would be less than attractive but, as long as care is exercised in planning and control is sensitive, we are not too concerned that other **small** farms will follow.

Coshletter means 'the base of the sloping mount' and there is indeed a long haul to the top! As a car driver, you will not be aware that this is the highest point on a main road in Skye, but cyclists believe it and the stagecoach drivers found *Sròn nan Aighean* the hardest part of the journey to *Dunvegan* and *Stein*. The farther slope, however, is a cyclists' dream!

The road now speeds down to another romantic intersection, *"The Fairy Bridge"*.

From here the road divides, left to *Dunvegan* and right to *Waternish*. We will first explore *Waternish* before going south-west to *Dunvegan*.

CHAPTER 5

The Vaternish (or Waternish) Wing
Wolves and Sheepskins

"O fàilt' air Rudha Bhatairnis
Gur maiseach leam do chluaintean
Thoir soraidh slàn gu Hàllain
'S nach fhaod mi thràigh a bhualadh."
I. Ferguson

"Oh welcome to Vaternish Point
Your plains are beautiful
Bear greetings to Hallin
As I cannot get to its shore."

As one might expect, *Fairy Bridge* is named from its legendary connection with the famous *Fairy Flag (An Bratach Sìth)*, which remains the treasured property of the MacLeods of Dunvegan. There was not always a bridge here. The Gaelic name for this important crossing point is *Beul-Atha nan Tri Allt* (The confluence of the Three Burns), as three significant streams converge nearby to form the Bay River.

Long ago, an early Chief of the Clan married a Fairy and they were blissfully happy. They had a baby son of whom both parents were proud. When the child was one year old, his mother announced to her husband that she must return to her own people but that the lad could remain in the human world until he was fully grown, when she would return for him. MacLeod was devastated, but knew better than to fight the inevitable lest the child be taken immediately. He agreed to accompany his wife from the Castle along the road. At the Ford, having kissed her loved ones goodbye, she presented the Chief with a silk sheet in which to wrap their baby son. She informed him that this would be their only means of communication and should be used sparingly. In times of famine, it would bring herring to the loch; in times when a MacLeod heir was required, it would bring fertility to the marriage bed and, in times of war, it would multiply the numbers of MacLeod warriors in the eyes of their enemies.

This is of course only one of several versions of the legend.

When Sir Reginald MacLeod of MacLeod (27th Chief) decided to have the flag mounted in a sealed glass case for protection and display, an expert from the Victoria and Albert Museum was called. Mr Mace's scientific and historical deductions concluded that the flag was indeed pure silk from the Middle East and that it was probably the famous banner of the sagas, *Landoda* (the Land Ravisher) which Harald Haardrada, the Norseman, had looted from the Pilgrim routes in Crusader times. Harald was killed at the Battle of Stamford Bridge in 1066 before most of his men had disembarked from his ship. It is known that he had several Hebrideans on the crew, who probably brought the banner north. Sir Reginald's reply was; *"You may believe that Mr. Mace, but I know that it was given to my ancestor by the fairies."* Mr. Mace replied; *"I bow to your superior knowledge."*

There are no buildings at *Fairy Bridge* now – only the multi-coloured recycling bins – and there was no church here in the 1840s when huge numbers flocked from all over Skye to listen to the preaching of Rev Roderick MacLeod of *Snizort*. Indeed a church would have been superfluous, as the numbers that gathered could be measured in thousands rather than hundreds. An eye witness in 1842 said; *"I saw the young and old, male and female, pouring forth from all sides of the land, from hills, and valleys, villages, hamlets and lonely huts. The loch too was covered with about fifty skiffs, like the multitudes which dotted the sea of Tiberias, in pursuit of the Lord himself when He was manifest in the flesh."*

Nowadays it is hard to believe the distances that people of all ages were prepared to walk to these services. No doubt there were shortcuts through the hills and there would be good company, but to walk to *Fairy Bridge* from *Braes, Glenmore* and *Portree*, which many did, is truly astonishing.

Maighstir Ruaraidh's support of the Free Church, which became popular with 'ordinary' people in 1843, led to a backlash from some landowners who supported the 'Established Church', over which they continued to have some influence. In 1846 at least 16 families in his congregation were ejected from their holdings. In 1847 a further 30 families received notices to quit. This evidence was given to a House of Commons Select Committee on 12th May 1847. Although many of those evicted were the sub-tenants of tacksmen or 'gentlemen farmers' in the parish, all were, directly or indirectly, the responsibility of Lord MacDonald. Whether or not the noble lord or only his factor had signed the orders is immaterial.

The first Free Church Minister of Bracadale, Rev. John Finlayson, had to fulfil his pastoral duties for a year, by walking to and from Portree, a distance of 24 miles, as he was refused accommodation in the parish!

There were buildings close to *Beul-Atha nan Tri Allt* in the distant past, however. Just a mile or so downstream from *Fairy Bridge*, protected by fairly deep gorges on two sides and the remains of a defensive wall on another, are a number of beehive cells and perhaps a fort and/or church. Suggestions are that this is a Neolithic defensive site which was later used as a place of worship. Boswell visited here and was informed by his guide, Rev Dr Donald MacQueen, that this was the *Temple of Anaitis,* a Syrian goddess, and that the presence of water on all sides was typical of sites dedicated to this deity. Dr Johnson, who was too rotund to reach the spot, but none the less, gave his opinion, said *"It may be a place of Christian worship, as the first Christians often chose remote and wild places to make an impression on the mind."* The Gaelic name *Teampan na h'Annait* seems to have been the cause of the confusion; *Annait* meaning mother-church. The distinguished archaeologist W. Douglas Simpson believes that this is probably *"the most ancient ecclesiastic foundation in the district and, beyond doubt, one of the most important primitive Christian sites in the Hebrides".*

Perhaps when the present forestry felling operations are complete, visitors will again have better access to *Annait*.

Let us now continue our journey through the *Waternish* or *Vaternish Wing*. The Norse name means *'watery promontory'* but the often quoted belief that it was so named because *"it is washed by Atlantic waves on three sides"*, could apply to any of Skye's *Wings*. On a dreich autumn morning, after a night of heavy rain, I sailed around Waternish. The large number of waterfalls and cataracts which tumbled down the precipitous cliffs, forming the headland, have convinced me that the Vikings named the peninsula from its abundance of fresh water, and not from the salt water which washes its coasts.

This *Wing* has seen much Clan warfare and troublous times, but is now a much sought-after abode for those who wish to escape the rat-race of our cities. There is indeed much beauty to enjoy, splendid views, superb wildflowers, coastal and moorland walks, as well as a wealth of history.

The first township on our route is called *Bay*. The four holdings on this fertile area were among the first of the new 'crofts' suggested by the Government in the wake of the 1912 Report of the recently appointed Crofters Commission.

The flourishing properties of *Camuslusta* and *Lusta*, perched as they are above *Loch Bay*, have the benefit of full sun and superb vistas. *Lusta* comes from a Gaelic word meaning 'flowery well' and this is indeed a delightful place in all seasons, when the weather is kind.

Donald MacKillop, a native of Berneray, has written a lovely poem in praise of this part of *Waternish*.

"Ri taobh Coill' an Fhàsaich	"Down by *Coill' an Fhàsaich*
Feasgar àghmhor leam fhìn	For a walk on a fine evening
Bha na h-eòin air na crannaibh	The birds sang in the trees
'S iad ri 'caithream gu binn	Full of joy and life.
Gun robh sìth air an Eilean	Skye was tranquil all around me
Fad sheallaidh mun cuairt	As far as I could see

'*S bha mo smuaint air mo chàirdean*	And so my thoughts turned to my friends
A bha tàmh leam ann uair."	Who once lived with me there."

Human habitation in *Waternish* is confined to the coastal strips and the bulk of the landmass forms rough moorland grazing along the backbone of the promontory.

On the hillside above, and north to *Dun Hallin,* we can still see evidence of wolf-traps cut into the slopes, and tales are told of the rescue of a trapper who had fallen in. His life was saved by his quick-thinking companion who managed to catch the wolf by his tail and to hold on long enough to allow him to reach safety. This wild landscape was the last area of Skye in which these predators were found, being eventually killed off in 1743. Foxes now remain as our largest mammalian predator, if we discount man!

Waternish, in the early 20th century, had its Dr Dolittle character in Captain MacDonald of Waternish House. In the garden he had a large menagerie of creatures, from otters to otter-hounds as well as tame herons, deer and peregrine falcons. He was said to have trained two golden eagles for hunting. Regarded as "*a keen naturalist and sportsman*" we are told by MacCulloch that, "*indoors are many rare, stuffed specimens, shot, often after days of watching, by the captain's unerring gun.*" I would suggest, on this evidence, that the term '*predator*' is more appropriate in this case than either '*naturalist*' or '*sportsman*'!

Was it Waternish House or another of the residences of the aristocracy which the bard, Donald MacLeod *(Dòmhnall nan Oran),* mentions in his poem '*Oran Aitreamh Ruairi*' penned in 1802?

"'*S ann an Steinn a thog thu 'n aitreamh* *Anns am faighte ghloinne lionta* *Ruma glas is fion na Frainge*	"It was in Stein you built your mansion Where the flowing glass was to be got Grey rum and wine from France

Uisgebeatha 's branndaidh riomhach	Whisky and costly brandy
Gheibhinn ann gach seorsa bidh	I would get there all manner of food
Chan urrain mi dhoibh 'ga chunntas	
Cruithneachd is briosgaidean Innseach	Wheat and Indian biscuits
Muc 'ga sgriobadh 's muilt 'g an ruagadh."	Pigs scraped and wedders dispersed."

Our road comes suddenly to a T-junction at the former property of Captain MacDonald and we go left to the quaint village of *Stein*. One could be forgiven for thinking that the through-road from Skye's portal at Kyleakin had been built for the sole purpose of conveying visitors to the welcoming sea-food restaurants along the bay at *Stein*, but this is a fairly recent delight. *Stein Inn* claims to be very ancient, but the village itself, laid out as a single street, was planned and built in 1787 by the British Fisheries Society. The previous year, a certain John Knox had visited Skye to assess its potential with regard to setting up fishing stations to provide food for the nation. His conclusions seem to have been arrived at solely from discussions with the proprietors and middleclass, and an assumption that fish would always be present in enormous shoals. Unfortunately his less than scientific study produced over-optimistic expectations.

"The great wealth of Sky consists in its marine productions. Here are at least twenty bays or lochs, which are occasionally frequented by herrings, and where many cargoes have been procured by vessels from the ports of Clyde, but none by the natives, because they have no vessels wherein to cure them.

"The lakes are frequented by salmon, mackerel, white and shell fish. Without, in the ocean, there are many excellent banks, of which the natives, from the want of stout wherries or decked vessels, are not able to avail themselves. Amidst this profusion of fish, in all their varieties, the utmost exertion of the people seems only to procure supplies for their own families, and a small quantity of cod, of inferior size and indifferently cured; which, as before observed, they sell or exchange for necessaries. When foundations shall be laid for the growth of three or four towns, and when the period arrives which will facilitate fisheries around this great island, by means of decked vessels, well provided with salt, cask, and experienced curers, the value of Sky will be found to exceed belief. To the navy it will be able to spare

1,000 seamen in every war, which at the rate of 200 seamen for every ship of the line, will be sufficient to navigate a little squadron, with men inured to hardships, and fearless of dangers."

On the strength of Knox's analysis, the village of *Stein* was built, salt, barrels and curers were brought in, and Skye's first real road, apart from cart tracks, was surveyed and engineered in 1799. This original main road ran from *Kylerhea* via *Broadford, Sligachan, Bracadale* and *Dunvegan* to *Stein*. After a few years, it was realised that the fickle behaviour of the herring shoals and the high cost of curing-salt meant that reliance on the West Coast fishing industry was not to be the answer to all the nation's wishes. A brick-works was opened at *Bay*, but the necessity of importing coal as fuel meant that this industry was also a disappointment and *Stein* once more reverted to a sleepy crofting township.

This area was another from which emigrant ships left for the new world carrying the cream of Skye's sons and daughters.

In the late 1960s, as I was growing up in *Portree*, a new phenomenon appeared in our island, causing quite a stir. The pop star Donovan had bought property at *Stein* as well as the *Island of Isay* in the bay. His group of assorted 'hangers-on' seemed to expand and contract over the years, as they sought 'the good life' and then realised that work 'is a four-letter word'. When the sun shone, life was indeed *'Mellow Yellow'* but some became only too keen to *'Catch the Wind'* and return to the 'crap of city life', as one of them described the alternative.

These days there is one of those ubiquitous fish-farms in *Lochbay* and, in summer, the tourist yachts provide a lovely spectacle as they anchor where once King *Haakon's* longships sought shelter on their return from defeat at the Battle of Largs.

The township of *Hallin,* from the Norse meaning the sloping field, is appropriately named and sits beneath the double-walled *Broch* of that name, *Dun Hallin*. Although not as well preserved as the *Dun Beag* at *Struan*, a great deal of skill and patience must have gone into the careful construction of the courses of stone work.

Two miles out into the bay to the west, lie the islands of *Isay* and *Mingay*. In geological terms they are very different. *Isay*, like most of the north Skye mainland, is composed of basalt sheets punctuated with dykes of dolerite. *Mingay* has exposed Jurassic limestone which underlies the igneous rocks. The alkaline limestone makes parts of *Mingay* appear green and fertile and the ruins of a limekiln confirm that in the past, use was made of this resource for agricultural purposes.

Isay has a more turbulent history.

About 1511 a dispute arose between the MacLeods of Raasay and the MacKenzies of Kintail, as a consequence of which the then Raasay Chief, *John Macgilliechallum* or *Ian an Tuaidh* (John of the Axe) was murdered in 1568 along with his male heirs by his brother-in-law *Ruaraidh 'Nimheach' Mhic Ailein*, Roderick 'the Venomous' MacLeod. The murder occurred on *Isay* after the Raasay MacLeods were tricked into attending a conference to discuss clan matters. Unfortunately for Roderick, one of the Chief's sons had been fostered out to the home of a renowned warrior Malcolm MacNeil. It seems that the Clan Chiefs required their insurance policies just as we do!

Such internecine strife seems to have amused Clan Donald, as one of their bards alludes to the incident in a rowing song or *iorram*.

"An tulgadh seo gu Eilean Iosaidh,	"This rocking to the Isle of Isay,
Far an d'rinn MacLeòid an dinear,	Where MacLeod made the dinner,
Far an d'rinn MacAilein diobart;	Where the son of Allan perpetuated
	an extirpation,
Dhoirt e fuil, 's gun chaisg e iotadh."	He shed blood and slaked his thirst."

Blood-thirsty times indeed! Some 40 years later, the son of Judge Morrison of Lewis, having enjoyed the hospitality of

Clan MacLeod at Dunvegan Castle, raided *Isay* and killed three of the clan. He was pursued and overtaken in the Minch. A hasty gallows was made from three oars, and he and his men were hanged at *Ardmore Point*. Swift justice!

It is said that, from this incident, the hill was given its name *Cnoc a' Chrochaidh*, the Hanging Hill. In a rock crevice, beneath the spot where the Lewismen were permitted to have a last prayer, several silver coins were discovered, dated 1604. It is believed that they were hidden there as a last gesture of defiance against the enemy.

When Dr Samuel Johnson and his colleague James Boswell visited here in 1775, the then Chief at Dunvegan, Norman ('The General') offered the ownership of *Isay* to Johnson on condition that he would agree to spend three months of the year on the island. Initially, the idea took his fancy. He imagined it would be grand to be its owner, to fortify it with cannon and to *"sally forth and take the Isle of Muck"*. Intrigued by the knowledge that landowners in the Highlands were often named after their properties it accorded him great satisfaction for Boswell to propose the toast; *"Isay – your health!"*

How many Highland landowners and potential landowners since have relished these feelings only to be beguiled by the counter-attractions of the south? Perhaps the 'three month per year' occupancy condition of ownership would be a good one for the 21st Century!

It was 'The General' himself who, very tellingly, said of his own class: - They are *"sucked into the vortex of the nation and lured to the capitals, they degenerate from patriarchs and chieftains to landlords; and they become as anxious for the increasing of rents as the new-made lairds, the novi homines, the mercantile purchasers of the lowlands."*

Dr Johnson also made the observation. *"Their chiefs being now deprived of their jurisdiction have already lost much of their influence, and as they gradually degenerate from patriarchal rulers to rapacious landlords, they divest themselves of the little that remains."*

At *Hallin* we now go east to *Knockbreck*. When I returned to Skye as Assistant Principal Teacher of Guidance at Portree High School in 1980, it was my pleasant duty to liase with all our 21 Associated Primary Schools on Skye and Raasay. This involved an annual visit to each, in order to meet the Primary 7 pupils who were soon to join us at the High School. What a delightful springtime outing! Among my favourite schools was *Knockbreck Primary*. Perched on the hill between *Hallistra* and *Gillen* it seemed such a busy yet peaceful workplace in its splendidly isolated position. Teacher and pupils in perfect harmony but pleased to welcome their visitors. During my career I was to discover that the vast majority of these youngsters, from all the schools, were a credit to their parents, their island and a joy to work with.

To get to *Gillen* (Norse word meaning ravine or narrow glen) we must go right at the junction and we will drive on to the road-end.

It's perhaps time for a walk in the fresh air to enjoy some more *Loch Snizort* views. The circular route to the *Cliffs of Score Horan* will just take about an hour and a half and, if the weather is fair, will lift the spirits as we enjoy the beauty that surrounds us. (Make sure you have a suitable map, walkers' guide and are clothed for the conditions! A good Skye guidebook is recommended in Appendix 2).

If we are lucky we will spot a kestrel or two and perhaps a hen-harrier along the route but, soaring above these cliffs golden eagles are very often to be seen, as they hunt for rabbits, hares and mice.

Sit awhile and admire the prospect!

You will be awed by the scenery, but please also pause to consider some aspects of our history.

Think back to Emigration times when Uig, the little port on the shore opposite was often a departure point!

One historian wrote; "*An emigrant ship would come into the loch by night and next morning a whole township would be found tenantless, its inhabitants having embarked to seek their fortunes beyond the sea in lands where they should only 'again in dreams behold the Hebrides'."*

"During the last week of July 1840 a full rigged ship and a brig left Loch Snizort for Prince Edward Island. The ship contained 400 people and the brig 200. The brig crossed in 31 days while the ship, due to poor navigation and losing its way, took 8 weeks. During the journey 9 passengers died on board and four or five babies were born."

"On July 6th 1841 the 1660-ton sailing ship 'Washington' with a complement of 850 passengers departed from Uig, Skye. The crossing was completed in a record 22 days, arriving at Charlottetown, PEI on July 28th where morning and evening worship were held on the Sabbath Day."

These trips were fairly normal but there were the occasions when fever broke out on the crowded ships or the weather was unfavourable. Sometimes conditions must have been horrendous!

At the Museum of the Isles at Armadale there is a very thought provoking notice:-

"Imagine you are lying in a space not much bigger than a large double bed. You are not on your own. You share this space, a glorified bunk, with your whole family. Either side of you, stretching away into the distance, there are other bunks. There are more above you, just a few feet away. At the foot of your bunk, across a passageway, there is another double row of bunks. It is dark and stuffy. The air smells. There are too many people crammed into a small dark space. You are on an emigrant ship, sailing away to a new life in Australia or North America."

"As a child, Donald Martin of Monkstadt was deeply saddened as he heard the wailing of those on board. 'I watched that ship as she sailed away, and ever since and now, I have asked myself and others, the reason why'."

How delighted these emigrants must have been to make land-fall. But excitement and anticipation soon waned in the cases of many. A Canadian, Dundas Warder wrote of these people:

"We have been pained beyond measure for some time past to witness in our

streets so many unfortunate Highland emigrants, apparently destitute of all means of subsistence, and many of them sick from want and other attendant causes. It was pitiful the other day to view a funeral of one of these wretched people. It was, indeed, a sad procession. The coffin was constructed of the rudest material; a few rough boards nailed together was all that could be afforded to convey to its last resting-place the body of a homeless emigrant. Children followed in the mournful train; perchance they followed a brother's bier, one with whom they had sported and played for many a healthful day among their native glens. Theirs were looks of indescribable sorrow. They were in rags; their mourning weeds were the shapeless fragments of what had once been clothes. There was a mother, too, among the mourners, one who had tended the departed with anxious care in infancy, and had doubtless looked forward to a happier future in this land of plenty. The anguish of her countenance told too plainly these hopes were blasted and she was about to bury them in the grave of her child."

This sad situation was not the case for all the emigrants of course, and some did exceedingly well in their adopted homelands, but Calum MacLeod of *'Calum's Road'* fame tells us of a conversation he had with John, the youngest son of Malcolm MacLeod who was evicted from *Manish*, Raasay (*Math-innis* means 'good pastures'). John, who had been six years old when the family emigrated in 1864, had returned for a visit to this country in 1934. Calum's father asked the visitor how the majority of the one thousand emigrants from this area had got on. He replied: *"Those evicted from Raasay that did well and attained the allotted span (70 years) I could count on my five fingers. Some died on the voyage. Of those who arrived, first, the aged died broken-hearted. Those younger, grief, a terrible voyage and hard work shortened their lives. Some were murdered, others drowned."* John himself had been one of the fortunate ones who had succeeded in business and had sufficient means to make a return visit to his birthplace.

Below the cliffs at *Loch Losait* the ruined houses, which now only provide shelter for sheep, bear testimony to the removal of those who once peopled these townships.

"*Chì mi cuimhneachan sgrìobht'*	"I see written memorials to those who
Air an linn nach eil beò	have gone.
Anns gach tobht' agas gàrach	In the old ruined walls
Gach càrn agus crò	Of each cairn and fold.
Anns gach àirigh th' air monadh	The sheiling in the hill
Agus caraidh th' air tràigh	And the caraigh by the shore
Nach gach leughadh le coigreach	Can't be read by the stranger
Mu'n chuideachd a dh 'fhàg."	About those who have left."

D.MacKillop

But our reason for taking this short walk was to raise the spirits and not depress them!

Hopefully the scent of the pines and wildflowers and some glimpses of wildlife will renew the spring in our steps.

Let us join the track, which will take us back to the turning area and our vehicle.

Our next destination is *Geary* (sheiling or enclosure). When viewed from *Uig* and *Earlish* across the water, the houses of Geary appear to be in danger of slipping down the steep fields to plummet over the high cliffs into the sea. This is another typical Skye township with a mixture of actively worked crofts, holiday homes and self-catering cottages. All too many of these houses however, have no lights of a winter evening, as the owners have fled south to work or hibernate!

Beneath us we see the *Ascrib* Group which lies between Skye's *Vaternish* and *Trotternish Wings*. They form a chain of five islands with various other tidal rocky outcrops. They were recently declared by the EU, along with *Isay* and *Loch Dunvegan*, to be a Special Area of Conservation owing to their breeding colonies of Common Seals. The Grey or Atlantic Seal is actually commoner than the Common Seal in these parts! Common seals are best distinguished from their cousins by their profiles while sunbathing on the rocks. They look like bananas!

There is only one house on the *Ascribs*; on the largest and most southerly island. The whole group was purchased by Lord Palumbo when they came up for sale in the late 1990s. He is a **Conservative Life Peer**, former chair of 'The Arts Council' and father of James 'Jamie' Palumbo, multi-millionaire owner of the "Ministry of Sound" record label and nightclub, and a well-known **Labour Party** supporter!

This whole coast is alive with seabirds, corvids and raptors and the place-names of the rocks, cliffs and promontories tell us that this has long been the case. *Creag An Fhithich* (Raven's Rock), *Caisteal an Fhithich* (Raven's Castle), names not surprising, as ravens were venerated by the Vikings (Odin's messenger). *Biod a' Choltraiche* (Razorbill's Peak) and *Biod Sgiath Na Corra-gribich* (Peak of the Heron's Wing) are typical. Guillemots, Razorbills, Puffins and Fulmars, nest on the cliffs and islands and provide interest for ornithologists and amateurs alike. One large rock, formed from a dolerite dyke, looks uncannily like an elephant and often has cormorants and shags diving off its tail, while Razorbills whiten its eye-socket with their guano!

Having satisfied our interest in *Waternish's* eastern side we turn at the *Geary* road-end and drive back to *Hallin* where we turn right and onto the low road to *Ardmore*.

"O nach prìseil leam Halainn
Sios gu bàgh na h-Aird Mhóir
Air a tràigh bha sinn daonnan
Cheart cho aotrom ri eòin
Ach a nis chan eil mànran
Fealla-dhà ann no spòrs
'S far do chluich sinn air leachdan
An diugh caidlidh na ròin."

"I think of Hallin beautiful
As it sweeps to Ardmore
We played carefree on the shore there
As happy as the birds
But now there's no joking
No laughter or fun
And the seals laze on the rocks
Where we used to play."

D. MacKillop

From here the 132 Kilovolt powerlines, which have traversed Skye, (mercifully without pylons) all the way from *Kylerhea,* now cross the Minch to supply the Western Isles with electricity. Very soon we envisage that power produced in the islands by wind, wave and tide will travel in the opposite direction to supply the rest of the country.

Ardmore was traditionally the home of Clan MacLeod's armourers; blacksmiths whose skills produced the two-handed Claymores (*Claidheamh Mòr,* Big Sword), *"When a man did strike with them he was obliged to apply both hands to the haft".*

In this part of Waternish there were at least two bloody clan battles and incidents in connection with each have become confused in the telling. *Beinn a' Ghobainn* commemorates one of these blacksmiths who fought valiantly in one of these battles against an equally powerful warrior of Clan MacDonald. We are told that the smith's wife intervened, seeing that her man was tiring. "Turn to me", she shouted to the enemy. This was sufficient to distract him long enough for the MacLeod to thrust him through. In this same battle, *Ruairaidh Unish* (Roderick son of Iain MacLeod of Unish), had slain many MacDonalds until his legs were cut off at the knees by a mighty sword swipe. He continued to fight on his stumps until loss of blood weakened him. His bravery was remembered at *Cnoc Mhic Iain* (the knoll of Iain's son), where a cairn still stands, by the *Crois Bhan* (the white cross), now long disappeared. It is supposed that this Battle of Vaternish of 1530 is the one remembered in the beautiful MacCrimmon *pìobaireachd* of that name. Seton Gordon, who was an authority on bagpipe music, tells us that another equally famous tune was composed on the death of the head of the family who occupied *Roag* in *Ardmore;* "Lament for MacSwan of Roag". I had assumed that that family had lived at the better known *Roag* in *Duirinish.*

The other, more famous battle at *Trumpan* and *Ardmore* occurred in the time of Norman, 12th Chief of the MacLeods of Dunvegan. He was an exceptionally cruel man in an age of cruelty. Unsure of the security of his position as chief, he massacred all who were potential rivals. This was not sufficient to put his mind at rest but, fearing assassination, he chose twelve bodyguards to protect him at all times. In order to qualify for the task, these men had to be experts in all the fitness-arts of 'The Games'; wrestling, leaping, caber-tossing and putting the stone. A further test was demanded for inclusion in this elite band. Each must be able to wrench off, with one hand, a bull's leg at the knee. For this reason, the twelve were named *"Na Buannachan"* (The Bullies).

It was in the time of this evil chief (1577) that the Clan MacLeod perpetrated the Massacre of the MacDonalds in the Isle of *Eigg*. 395 persons, men, women and children were suffocated in a cave, on that island, to which they had fled for safety.

These people were a branch of the MacDonalds of ClanRanald who at that time owned the islands of *Uist*. Revenge was called for and plans were prepared!

The following year, on a Sunday in early May, while many MacLeods were worshipping in the *Trumpan* Church, dedicated to St Conan, a band of MacDonalds, with eight *birlinns* (war galleys) from *Uist* made a daring raid on *Waternish*, landing at high tide, hidden by fog at *Ardmore Bay*. Quickly they surrounded the building and fired the thatched roof. The single door was barricaded, and the windows, being less than four inches wide, made escape impossible. No doubt the anguished cries of the men and women would have been answered by injunctions to remember *Eigg*! Perhaps the MacDonald piper would have played a scornful tune! Yet one woman, although badly mutilated, was able to escape, probably through the burning roof, to raise the alarm, before she succumbed to her injuries at *Sloc Mairearaid* (Margaret's Hollow).

All the able-bodied men from miles around gathered to fight off the invaders who were now jubilantly rounding up the MacLeods' cattle. Their efforts were largely ineffective but sufficiently delayed the enemy so that their galleys became stranded by the retreating tide. A local tailor, whose archery skills were legendary, pinned the MacDonald's down by making each arrow count. We are told that marks on a nearby rock were made by his women helpers, who sharpened each arrowhead for its purpose.

Word of the tragedy had meanwhile reached *Dunvegan* Castle. The clan was called to arms, the Fairy Flag was brought from its iron chest and the fleet sailed the short distance to *Ardmore*. As the famous banner was unfurled, *"the very blades of grass appeared as fighting men to the eyes of Clan Ranald"*. When the last of the MacDonalds had been killed, their bodies were laid out along the line of the earth dyke, which had kept the sea from encroaching on the arable fields of *Ardmore*. To avoid the task of burial, the dyke was simply overturned to cover the corpses. Hence the name *'Blar Milleadh Gàraidh',* (Battle of the Destruction of the Wall) has been applied to this tragic incident.

Surrounded by its ancient cemetery, the well preserved gable and one wall of *Ardmore* Church still remains a reminder to us of the evil of revenge.

The baptismal font, reputed never to be dry, was pointed out to me, at the churchyard gate by my teachers in 1968. On my last visit, recently, I failed to find it.

The ancient pewter communion chalice from this church is safe in the Museum of Island Life at *Kilmuir*.

Close to the remaining wall of the church is the grave of Rachel Ann Erskine wife of a Lord Justice Clerk of Edinburgh, interred here in May 1745. She is actually buried here although she had two other false funerals, attended and sanctioned by the nobility. Boswell says: *"The true story of this lady is as frightfully romantic as if it had been the fiction of a gloomy fancy"*.

This lady, Lady Grange, was an ardent Protestant and Hanovarian supporter. Her husband, James Erskine, Lord Grange, was a brother of the Earl of Mar and he was a secret Jacobite. Mar, known as 'Bobbing John', had changed sides on a number of occasions but eventually had led the unsuccessful Jacobite Rebellion of 1715. From this time on, certain noblemen, particularly in Scotland, continued to plan for the restoration of the Stuarts to the British Throne. Lord Grange's home became a meeting-place for those Jacobites among whom were Norman MacLeod 22nd Chief of MacLeod, Sir Alexander MacDonald 15th Chief of MacDonald and Simon Fraser of Lovat. Following a meeting of the conspirators on the evening of 22nd January 1732, Lady Grange threatened to reveal the details which she had overheard. Believing that she was certainly capable of bringing the plot to the attention of the Government, a plan to silence her was quickly drawn up by her husband and the others. Next morning a funeral notice appeared to the effect that Lady Grange had died suddenly and would be buried in the Greyfriars' Churchyard. The funeral was well attended but the coffin only contained clods and stones. Meanwhile Rachel was taken under cover of night, by representatives of the MacDonald and MacLeod clans to *Castle Tioram* in Morar. It was soon realised that no place on the mainland would be safe and that, if their plans were exposed, many important Highlanders would be charged with treason. Lady Grange was moved first to MacLeod territory in *Duirinish* but managed to send a message to her friends, hidden in a skein of wool. As suspicions had been raised in high places, the prisoner was quickly taken to the lonely Island of *Heiskeir* which belonged to the MacDonalds and, after two years, to MacLeod's more remote *St. Kilda*. The Chiefs were now well and truly implicated and open to blackmail!

In *St. Kilda* she had to endure extreme privations for one used to the fine foods and comforts of Edinburgh society. She had to get used to the sea-bird diet of the inhabitants and found it very difficult to communicate with the islanders as she understood no Gaelic, and they, no English. For seven years she remained on the *"vile and neasty stinking, poor isle"* as she described it. Through the good offices of a visiting island missionary she had a message passed to her solicitor 'Hope of

Rankeillor', who set off by ship with 25 armed men to rescue her. The news was out! Lord Grange claimed that he had *"sequestrated his wife as a person of unsound mind, unfit to have the management of her family"*. Before Hope's ship arrived, she was quickly moved to the wilds of *Assynt* and then back to a cave near *Idrigill Point* in *Duirinish*. Eventually, her mind having given way, she was given some freedom and the charity of the local people near *Ardmore*. A certain Rorie MacNeill of Trumpan, according to *Dunvegan* Castle documents, was paid £33 .00s. 11^1/$_2$d (accommodation/hush money?) and, according to Rev. Donald Corbet, she was allowed an annual visit from her Lowland minister. On her death, a costly funeral was arranged at the *Kilmuir* cemetery near *Dunvegan* Castle but once again, the coffin was filled with clods and stones and the tragic Lady Grange was secretly buried at *Trumpan*!

It is difficult to understand why the farce was continued, even after her death, but documents reveal that the MacLeod Chief paid £30 .15s. 5d for the final arrangements. That year, of course was 1745 *Bliadhna a'Phrionnsa* (the year of the Prince) and MacLeod of MacLeod had recently become an MP! Politics can be very messy!

The following year, *Waternish* very nearly had another 'Romantic Visit'!

Early on Sunday 29th June, having set off in a six-oared boat from *Rossinish*, *Benbecula*, Flora MacDonald and Bonnie Prince Charlie, disguised as Betty Burke, attempted to land on the west of the *Vaternish* Wing. They hoped to take shelter from the storm then raging. On approaching a landing place, they noticed that it was occupied by soldiers and quickly rowed off. Shots were fired but no one was hit. Having swiftly rounded *Ruadha Bhatarnais*, they pulled into a cleft in the rocks for an hour, to eat some bread and butter, as ships of war could be seen passing by. When all was safe, they made haste towards *Monkstadt* in *Trotternish*. *(For their adventures in Trotternish – see 'Like a Bird on the Wing')*

Although almost a third of the landmass of *Vaternish* extends north from *Trumpan*, the road stops here. For the fit and healthy, the walk to *Ruadha Bhatarnais* (Waternish Point) is a pleasant one in good weather. (Allow 4 hours). You will pass *Cnoc Mhic Iain* and see two typical Skye brochs. The first, *Dun Borrafiach,* is well preserved, having walls of massive stones which still stand about three metres tall. *Dun Gearymore* is more of a ruin, but we can yet see a portion of passageway with its roof intact.

Another ruin close to the track is the former *Unish* House, once the home of the tacksmen of *Unish,* among whom was the notorious Norman MacLeod of *Unish* who was implicated in a plot in 1739 to abduct men and women from the islands in order to sell them as slaves in the American colonies. Norman was the son of a distinguished father, Donald MacLeod of Bernera, known as 'The Old Trojan'. He was a redoubtable warrior and, when his Chief failed to 'come out at the '45', he set out on his own to join the Prince. Donald married three times. *"In his 75th year, he married his third wife, by whom he had nine children. He died age 90 in 1783."* Three full brothers from this family, brought up at *Unish,* were destined to become Generals in the British Army. (Derek Cooper wrongly states that the family lived at *Hunish* house in Kilmuir, Trotternish.)

There is evidence that this, now deserted area, was occupied by a large population up to the late 19th century. In 1851, *Waternish* had 4 Church Schools, 12 teachers and 180 scholars. One of these Gaelic schools was at *Unish*. Its headteacher from 1839 to 1842 was another Norman MacLeod known as 'the Old Soldier' because he, as a young man, had fought fearlessly in the British Army. On his discharge he tells that, *"In Edinburgh I was struck by the bullet of Love"*, a reference to his conversion on hearing a Gaelic sermon by the well known *Lochcarron* minister Rev Lachlan MacKenzie. His school was a long thatched building with his home at one end and the classroom/meeting room at the other. His pupils were taught to read Gaelic. The Bible was their textbook. Teachers in these schools were warned not to hold religious meetings in opposition to the authorised clergy and a delegation from the local Presbytery was sent to admonish him. *"Why do you hold meetings here"*, he was asked. *"I do it for the glory of God"*, was the reply. The local people were told not to listen to him; saying disparagingly, *"He's only an old soldier"*. On several other occasions attempts were made by the authorities to stop his religious activities but to no avail. Unlike the ministers, he was held in great affection by the people and was supported by them after his retirement. He died in 1858 aged 84. On that morning, he had apparently told his wife, *"Before this day ends I will be with Donald Munro."*

Our tour now returns toward *Fairy Bridge*, passing once again through *Hallistra*, *Hallin* and *Lusta*. At *Hallin*, it is pleasing to know that a degree of co-operation now exists between two Presbyterian Churches which now share the Meeting House facilities. Perhaps in *Waternish*, long a place of war, we now see the beginning of a world-wide time when *"swords will be beaten into ploughshares and spears into pruning hooks"*. The delightful Skyeskyns business at *Brae Stein*, which adds value to local, hand-combed sheepskins provides a wonderful change in what was once the abode of the wolf.

CHAPTER 6
Of Castle and Coral

Otta Swire says that the road from *Fairy Bridge* to *Dunvegan* is *"a road of birds"*. Indeed this is true, but perhaps not any more so than other stretches of moorland road on Skye. The old name of this flat area is *Lian Airigh Nan Geadh* (the plain of the sheiling of the goose). Perhaps it is named after a domestic goose, as it was customary for crofters to take their hens, ducks and geese along with their cattle to the hill grazings in early summer, in order to allow the crops on the arable land to grow on unmolested by the farmyard stock. This transhumance to seasonal pasture grounds provided opportunities for appreciation of the beauties of nature. William Ross's delightful poem is a perfect illustration:

"Nuair thig a' Bhealltuinn,
'S an Samhradh lusanach,
Bidh sinn air àirigh
Air àird nan uchdanan;
Bidh cruit nan gleanntan,
Gu cainntir, cuirteasach,
Gu tric 'gar dùsgach
Le surd gu moch-eirigh."

"When Maytime comes,
And the leafy summer,
We will be in the sheiling
On the height of the braes;
The lyre of the glens,
Will be sweetest and dignified,
Often rousing us
With the joy of early morning."

In season, curlews, lapwings and golden plover are common here and skylarks bring joy to the early summer skies. The cuckoo delights us in May and early June but tradition says that on the death of a Chief of Clan MacLeod the cuckoo deserts

Dunvegan in order to carry the bad news to the islands of the *St Kilda* group, far out in the west.

These days, kestrels are the most common raptor to be spotted on the moor, as they pounce to take advantage of road-kill. The 'tourist eagle', often to be seen sitting on fence posts and telegraph poles is, of course, the common buzzard. Hen-harriers quarter the heather ground on the lookout for mice and voles and sparrow-hawks dart out from the tree shelter in pursuit of other little birds. Around the coast peregrine falcons seem not to be as common as they once were but, when we do spot one, it certainly is a joy. In a stoop they are the fastest creatures in the World!

The Royal Society for the Protection of Birds regards this area as a dispersal zone for young Sea Eagles and Golden Eagles and feared that these birds would be detrimentally affected by the new wind-turbines. To date there seems to be no evidence of a detrimental effect. Indeed there is no evidence of **any** bird kill from **any** wind farm in the UK! Perhaps the birds are wiser than their human friends give them credit for!

At *Horneval* (N. The fell of the eagle), the road bears right for *Dunvegan*. This north part of Skye was well known territory for two of the island's best known ornithologists, Seton Gordon and Rev. Hugh MacPherson. In 1968, I had good advice from Seton Gordon for an article on birds which I wrote for a school magazine entitled '*Skye '68*'. He was generous with his time and exceedingly helpful. His writings about his beloved Skye, its people, landscape, flora and fauna have inspired many. Part of his obituary in '*Scottish Birds*' reads:

"As with many fine naturalists, most details within his exceptional experience will have died with him. He was a masterly describer, of things in breadth, of incident, of anecdote. Detailed analytical research was not his way, and this is as true of his contributions on place names and history as on ornithology. However, analytical researchers and men interested in problems often fail to interest the layman, and seldom excite him as Gordon did for many. Future Scotsmen will read him when many of the analysts have been forgotten."

Hugh MacPherson belongs to an earlier period. He, reluctantly, inherited the *Glendale* Estate in 1881 and soon developed a love of Skye and a passion for its wildlife. His legacy as an absentee landlord is not positive, but as an observer and recorder of birds he was second to none. He recorded 153 species of birds seen by him on the island.

Our drive takes us past the two *Kilmuir* cemeteries, old and new, of this *Duirinish* parish. The old *Kilmuir* Church (St Mary's) was conferred on Sir Nichol Berchame in 1501 by James IV of Scotland as an annexe to the cathedral-church on *Eilean Chaluim Chille* (St. Columba's Isle at Skeabost). In the old cemetery are buried some of the more recent MacLeod Chiefs, including the well remembered Dame Flora 28th Chief, and the MacCrimmons, pipers to the Clan. Apparently the Standard Bearers were, by tradition, buried at Rodel in Harris, where many of the early Chiefs were laid to rest.

One other interesting gravestone commemorates a Thomas Fraser of Beaufort, Lord Lovat, married to Sibella, daughter of *Iain Mòr* the 16th Chief in 1699. *"For the great love he bore the family of MacLeod, he desired to be buried near his wife's relations, in the place where two of her uncles lay"*.

This church saw the tryst between a party of the Earl of Argyle's men and *Iain Dubh* the usurper, 11th Chief in 1558. The Campbells had been sent to assert the rights of Mary, only daughter of William the 9th Chief of MacLeod, as the rightful heir. Argyle aimed to marry her into his family in order to have a claim on MacLeod territory, but most of the clan were against female succession. *Iain Dubh* pretended to go along with the agreement as long as he could remain Chief for his lifetime. Papers were duly signed and the parties made their way to *Dunvegan* Castle to eat and drink. A sumptuous meal was served and the eleven men in the Campbell delegation were seated alternately with MacLeods around the large table. After several courses and many toasts, cups of blood were brought to the table. This was the signal for each MacLeod to slay his neighbour. The eleven Campbells perished, but some of their servants were able to reach their ships anchored at *Roag*, and escaped to tell the tale of treachery. Needless to say, Mary did not succeed but Argyle's second choice, Norman, third son of *Alastair Crotach*, became the 12th Chief and *Iain Dubh* was forced to flee to Ulster where his own cruelty was rewarded by the Chief of O'Donnell who had *"red-hot irons thrust through his bowels"*.

Although its name suggests an ancient Celtic origin, 'the fort of the few', or 'little fort', the earliest mention I can find of *Dunvegan* and its Castle is in connection with the progenitor of Clan MacLeod; *Leod*. In 1292 King John Balliol of Scotland made Skye part of the Sheriffdom which included *Glenelg* on the mainland and the islands of *Lewis*, the *Uists*, *Barra* and the *Small Isles*. At this time the MacLeods were already established in this area and held most of these lands under two families; *Siol Torquil* or MacLeods of Lewis and *Siol Tormod* or MacLeods of Harris. *Torquil* and *Tormod* were the two sons of *Leod* who in turn was the son of Olave the Black, King of Man, a Norseman. Some historians claim the name Lewis (Gaelic *Leòdhas*) is *Leod-Hus*, Norse for the home of *Leod*. It was on *Leod's* marriage to the only daughter of MacRaild, a Norse knight, that the four Wings of Skye came into his possession and he set up residence at MacRaild's Castle – *Dunvegan*. There are MacRaild families in Duirinish to this day and it is said that they claimed the protection of Clan MacLeod and were their Galley-builders at *Colbost* on the opposite shore of *Loch Follart* (now *Loch Dunvegan*) from the Castle.

Leod died about 1280 and was buried at Iona, as were the next six chiefs of the *Siol Thormoid*.

The foundations of Leod's original castle can still be identified and suggest that the only entrance at that time was by the Sea Gate which would have been guarded by barbican, yett and portcullis. More than 700 years later the same family are in residence – at least for part of the year! The Keep was built in the time of Malcolm the 3rd Chief, whose marriage had brought him into favour with King David II of Scotland, and so the Royal masons were employed. The Fairy Tower was added by the 8th Chief, Alastair '*Crotach*'. Following various additions over the years, a front door was first made in 1748 but could only be reached by a flight of stairs until the moat was eventually filled in to doorstep level. When Johnson and Boswell visited in September 1773 they encouraged the Chief and his Lady to *"keep to the rock; it is the very jewel of the estate. It looks as if it had been let down from heaven by the four corners, to be the residence of a Chief."* They also insisted that the Macleod family should – *"never leave Rory Mòr's cascade."* This reference was to the little waterfall called Rory Mòr's Nursemaid which lulled the 15th Chief to sleep at night and without whose lullaby he was unable to enjoy a complete night's rest. Both Dr Johnson in 1773 and Sir Walter Scott in 1814 enjoyed the murmuring of the cascade as they slept in the 'Fairy Room'.

Further remodelling of the Castle continued in 1790 and 1814 before the 'pseudo-baronial pepper-pot turrets' were added in Victorian times.

Nowadays this is the most visited building in Skye and benefits from extensive gardens planted in the late 1800s when it was said that the Castle grounds had examples of more than a third of British Flora. During Skye's hurricane of March 1921 over 40,000 trees were blown down or were subsequently felled.

In the 1960s, my father, who was an electrician, was called to do some electrical work at the Castle. He found that Dame Flora MacLeod, the then Chief (28th), although a redoubtable lady, was very charming, and had a ready sense of humour. On discovering that his surname was Macdonald, she asked, *"Are you not afraid we will lock you in the dungeon?"* "No! As long as you don't try to marry me to a MacLeod", was his reply. His response referred to an old tale where a MacDonald prisoner was supposedly offered the choice of marrying a rather ugly sister of an early

Chief, or the death penalty. The MacDonald's reply was, *"Give me the rope!"*

In far off times prisoners were lowered or, more likely, dropped into the 13 foot deep dungeon and left to die. The delicious smell of food, cooking in the kitchens, must have greatly added to the discomfort of their last days!

The other parts of the interior of the Castle are just as fascinating. History oozes from the walls! Many of the fine portraits of Chiefs, their Ladies and other family members were painted by famous artists. Sir Henry Raeburn, Sir William Beechey, Victor Erkhart, Guido Schmidt, Allan Ramsay and Henry W Pickersgill are all represented by some enormous canvases as well as delightful little studies.

In the Front Hall your attention is drawn to the Bull's Head in the archway, donated to Dame Flora in the 1950s. Attached is the ancient motto of the Clan, *"Hold Fast"*. I have heard three versions of how this slogan came to be associated with the MacLeods. The most likely tale involved the famous *Rory Mòr*. While out hunting with a retinue of his men, they were suddenly alerted, in the time-honoured fashion by signal fires on the surrounding duns, to the fact that their enemies, had landed in Loch Follart. Having no transport, the Chief quickly led his servants to a herd of cattle grazing nearby and, mounting the bull, ordered his men to do likewise and use their broad horns to "Hold Fast". Such was their skill, and the speed of the herd, that the enemies were routed before the Castle could be seized. The magnificent bull became a symbol for the Clan and, dying in a good old age, donated one of its horns to be *Rory Mòr's* Horn. This famous silver-mounted drinking horn, kept in the Drawing Room, has a capacity of a bottle and a half. Tradition says that the Chief's heir must consume a full horn of claret "without setting down or falling down", as a proof of manhood (or womanhood). I'm sure they are very glad that tradition does not specify Talisker whisky!

It was also *Rory Mòr* who was gifted the Dunvegan Cup by the O'Neills of Ulster for his support against Queen Elizabeth I of England in 1596. The cup is made from bog oak, later mounted in silver with corals and semi-precious stones and belonged to *Niall Glun Dubh* (Niall of the black knees, King of Ireland 916 – 919). *Sir Rory Mòr*, had become a national figure and was knighted by James VI and I in 1613, in exchange for good behaviour. In fact he was the only MacLeod Chief to be granted a knighthood. From that time the Castle became less of a fortress and more of a rich mansion. The Chiefs gradually began to see themselves as the aristocracy rather than the 'fathers of the family' (*Clann* means children) and spent much of their time in the south among their equals. The 17th Chief, Roderick (the Witty), impoverished the Castle by his gambling addiction.

It was traditional for the Chiefs to be sponsors of the Arts, and this practice continued with Clan MacLeod up until the time of the 18th Chief, *Iain Breac*, who was the last to sponsor a bard, a harpist, a jester and a piper. The tales of the *sennachie* or story-tellers were 'the history books' and 'news-bulletins' of the day and wandering minstrels were encouraged to visit the ancient halls.

"Bu bhinn caismeachd sgeòil,
Aig luchd astair,
Is ceòil na h-Eireann."

"Sweet was the progress,
Of the travelling people,
And the music of Ireland."

Màiri ni'n Alasdair Ruaidh (Mairi daughter of Red Alasdair) wrote these words in praise of the MacLeods and their hospitality. She was perhaps the most famous of the Bards of *Dunvegan*, who exerted a powerful influence to stir up the warriors to boldly fight against the enemy. Bravery was praised and cowardice scorned! So potent a force were the bards thought to be that the Government in their 'Regulations for Chiefs' sought to banish them because *"they defylit the haill isles"*.

From earliest times, the *clarsach* or Highland harp was the main musical instrument and the post of harpist was a very honourable one. The last harpist to the MacLeods was Roderick Morison *(An Clàrsair Dall)* the blind harpist.

The music of the harp, being more benign, was superseded by the music of the *Pìob Mhòr* (Highland bagpipe), which was more suited to times of clan warfare. It was often called the Great Highland War Pipe and was designed to strike fear into the hearts of the enemy while encouraging an adrenalin rush in the clansmen. (classic 'fight or flight' psychology). Indeed these tactics still proved effective during the World Wars.

Pìobaireachd, often corrupted to pibroch (literally meaning "pipering" or the actions of a piper), refers to the *Ceòl Mòr* (Great Music), as opposed to *Ceòl Beag* or (Little Music), and is the Classical Music of the Bagpipe. Ceòl Beag refers to jigs and reels, marches and airs; rhythmic tunes for marching or dancing, many of which also go back hundreds of years.

Ceòl Mòr **Laments** were composed as a result of sad events such as deaths or defeats in battle. **Salutes** are tunes that acknowledge a person, a location or an event. They were often written on the occasion of the birth of children or after a visit to, or by, a prominent figure such as a clan chief. **Gatherings** were tunes written specifically for a clan. These tunes were used to call a clan together by their chief. The tune structure is usually simple so that it could be recognized easily by clan members. **Rowing** Pibroch were more rhythmic tunes used to encourage and pace rowers, while crossing the sea. There were also **Satires** and **Hymns of Praise**.

Many Pibroch tunes have intriguing titles such as *'The Big Spree'*, *'Too Long in This Condition'*, *'The Unjust Incarceration'*, *'The Piper's Warning to His Master'*, *'Scarce of Fishing'* and *'The Desperate Battle of the Birds'*.

It is believed that every pibroch once had its own words but only one or two of these have survived.

One of the most moving tunes, with an equally moving story behind it, was composed by the master piper *Padruig*

Mòr MacCrimmon. It is *'The Lament for the Children'*. On one occasion a foreign ship dropped anchor in Loch Follart bringing the deadly disease of measles, which caused devastation among the population of Skye. Patrick had eight sons and all but one succumbed to the plague. The emotion and despair of the composer make this tune particularly poignant.

After the defeat of the Jacobite Army at Culloden in 1746, the Government banned "the bearing of arms and wearing of tartan". Included in the ban were the bagpipes as they were regarded as "instruments of war"!

As well as the Arts, early Science had its place in the courts of the Clan Chiefs. The MacBeth, Bethune or Beaton families were herbalists and even performed experimental surgery. They were the healers or physicians to the clans long before the distinguished MacLean family took on that role in Skye and elsewhere.

"Clann 'ic Bheatha a'ghnàth ghrinn, "MacBeths of the Polished ways,
Luchd snaidheadh chnàmh is chuislean." Men who slit bones and veins".

It has been suggested that the Gaelic name for Beaton is *MacBheathan* (the lifegiver) and that the family may have been involved in the profession in these islands since the 14th century. On the 1657 gravestone of a Dr Donald Beton, in the churchyard in *Iona* is a Latin inscription, which translated reads; *"Lo he falleth by the dart of victorious, unrighteous death – who himself so oft loosed others from their ills – to God alone be glory."*

Martin Martin tells us of: *"an illiterate empiric Neil Beaton in Skye, who of late is so well known in the isles and continent, for his great success in curing several dangerous distempers, though he never appeared in the quality of a physician until he arrived at the age of forty years, and then also without the advantage of education. He pretends to judge the various qualities of plants and roots by their different tastes; he has likewise a nice observation of the colours of their flowers, from which he learns their astringent and loosening qualities: he extracts the juice of plants and roots after a chymical way, peculiar to himself, and with little or no charge."*

There are also many tales of a Farquhar Beaton, *Fearchar Lighiche* (Farquhar the Healer) and his son *Niall Og*, who were in turn, physicians at *Dunvegan* Castle. *Fearchar* apparently understood the language of the Ravens!

Was it perhaps this Farquhar Beaton, or Bethune, who was commended for his distinction as a surgeon at the Battle of Worcester in 1651? The MacLeod Clan was represented in this battle by a very large army commanded by Sir Norman MacLeod of *Bernera* and Sir Roderick MacLeod of *Talisker*. Clan MacDonald also took part on the side of the Stuarts, supported by the Covenanting Parliament, but neither Chief marched south. Before setting off, the MacLeods from Skye and Harris gathered, 1000 strong, at the *Lag Buidhe* near *Ose*. In that defeat by Cromwell, over 700 warriors of Clan MacLeod were killed and many others were shipped as prisoners to the West Indies!

"Bha fios cò sibh,
Ann an iomartas rìgh,
'Nuair bu mhuladach strì
Theàrlaich."

"It is known who you were,
In the King's conflicts most tragic,
When Charles' struggle was most bitter."

The MacLeod poetess *Màiri ni'n Alasdair Ruaidh*, who composed these words in praise of the clan, had many more words of praise for her hero, Sir Norman, third son of Sir Rory Mòr, than any of the 'five lairds of MacLeod' in whose days she is supposed to have lived.

"Fear do chéille, 's do ghliocais,
Do mhisneach, 's do mheanmain,
Do chruadail, 's do ghaisge,
Do dhreach, is do dhealbha,
Agus t'-uaisle,
Cha bu shuarach ri leanmhuinn."

"One of thy prudence, thy wisdom
Thy courage and thy spirit,
One of thy hardihood and valour,
Thy mien and thy mould
Thy courage and thy nobility,
Were no trifle to trace."

Is it any wonder that she was banished from the Castle for a time? The chiefs must certainly have been jealous.

Nonetheless this hero's sword is now on display at Dunvegan Castle as it was gifted by his family to a later chief.

A tale is told that *Coinneach Odhar*, who may or may not have been the Brahan Seer of Clan MacKenzie, pronounced a prophecy on the future of Clan MacLeod, which goes as follows. *"When Norman, the fourth Norman (Tormod nan Tri Thormaid), son of the slender, bony English lady, shall perish by accidental death; when the MacLeod's Maidens shall become the property of a Campbell; when a fox shall have cubs in a turret of the Castle; when the Fairy Flag will be unfurled for the last time, then the glory of the Clan will depart and their lands be sold so that a coracle will be sufficiently large to carry all the gentlemen of MacLeod across the Loch; but in times far distant, an Iain Breac will arise to redeem the estates and raise the honour and power to a greater state than ever."*

Many are convinced that, at least the first part of the prophecy has been fulfilled.

In July 1799, unbeknown to the family, their business manager broke open the iron chest in which the Fairy Flag was then stored. Shortly after this event, Norman, the fourth of the name in a row, a lieutenant in the Royal Navy, was killed in an explosion on HMS Queen Charlotte. Orbost Estate, on which are MacLeod's Maidens, was sold to Angus Campbell of Ensay and surprisingly, a tame vixen belonging to the Lieutenant gave birth to cubs in the Castle's West Turret. All this some 200 years after the time of *Coinneach Odhar*.

A young *Iain Breac* who might have been the one to restore the Clan fortunes was a victim of World War I —killed in 1915.

Having spent much time on the fortunes of this historic building, it is time to drive off to the north. On our right we pass *Totachochaire*, the ruin of the cook's house, before seeing the *Fiadhairt* peninsula which, at one time, was used as a deer enclosure. *Dun an Iardhard*, a mile north of the Castle, is another good example of a broch. This one was excavated in 1914 and several relics were discovered. The most interesting was a terra-cotta model of a bale of goods wrapped in skins. This item is said to be of Roman origin, a type of offering usually laid on an altar to ensure success on a merchant's journey.

Both John MacCulloch and Douglas Simpson speak highly of the beauties of *Loch Follart* which is now, more commonly called *Loch Dunvegan*. MacCulloch writes, *"I must not however pass Loch Follart without pointing out the beauty of the views over its wide expanse sprinkled with islands; enhanced by the interest derived from the picturesque aspect of Dunvegan Castle."*

Simpson adds, *"Perhaps the blue waters of the Loch, with its emerald and russet islands, fringed by golden seaweed, the swart embattled cliffs that margin its rocky shores, the green or tawny slopes with their marvelous fragrant carpet of spring and summer flowers – perhaps all of these are matched elsewhere in Skye. But the singular outlines of MacLeod's Tables, like a pair of sinister couchant monsters, the far-off conical spires of Harris, the glittering coral sands below Claigan, and the dark umbrageous, sweetly-scented woods that embossom the hoary castle – these are the things that give Loch Dunvegan a character of its own."*

It is a joy to find that others, able to express themselves better than oneself, have also appreciated this glorious part of our island.

Perhaps another visitor on 31st August 1779 was not as appreciative of the beauties of *Loch Follart*. This Scots-born pirate, 'Father of the American Navy', and later to become 'Chevalier de France' and Rear Admiral in the Russian Navy, was here for a more sinister purpose. John Paul Jones in his ship the *Bonhomme Richard*, was intent on plundering the Castle, knowing that Norman the 23rd Chief was on military duty in America. However, Jones' plans were thwarted by the appearance of a long, piper-led procession on the loch-side road, winding its way to the cemetery at Kilmuir for the burial of the tacksman of *Suardal*. The vast crowd of mourners had seemed like clansmen on the march.

Although no beacons had been lit on this occasion, the seven Duns around the Loch were afire again in 1789 for the homecoming of the Chief, who had risen to the rank of General during his campaigns in America and India. All the important cadets of the Clan were gathered to welcome Norman, hoping that the wealth that he had accumulated would be sufficient to buy back the estates which the MacLeods had been forced to sell in his absence. Expectations were high and the MacCrimmon piper played '*Rory Mòr's Salute*'.

Norman 'the General' was a popular Chief who, according to Pennant, *"feels for the distresses of his people, and insensible of his own, with uncommon disinterestedness has relieved his tenants from oppressive rents, has received, instead of the trash of gold, the treasure of their warm affections and unfeigned prayer."*

His own words, *"I would rather drink punch in the house of my people, than be enabled by their hardships to have claret in my own"*, are indeed noble sentiments, but the decline of the Clan continued. Unfortunately, this highly principled individual eventually failed himself and his people by losing a large proportion of his £100,000 fortune, like his grandfather, to a gambling addiction.

His son John Norman said of him, *"He was the first of his family to part with his inheritance and he was doubly grieved to find that he had impoverished his heirs without materially benefiting himself."*

We next come to *Claigean* (the Cultivated Place) and then, on foot, to our Coral Beach. Unlike the Western Isles, Skye does not have the beautiful golden sands which have been formed by the power of the Atlantic waves but we do have this beach which was for long believed to be the only coral beach in Britain. Rather disappointing then, to find that, unlike the true coral sands of the Caribbean, this beach is formed from bleached fragments of a type of seaweed called *Lithothamnion Corallioides*. Sparkling white in the sunshine, it appears no less beautiful in spite of this knowledge. From here we look across the *Little Minch* to the *Sound of Harris*. Clan MacLeod had fortresses on the *Isle of Pabbay* in the *Sound* and of course at *Rodel* on the southern tip of *Harris*. One of their ablest Chiefs, both in peace and war, was *Alastair Crotach* (Alexander the Hunchback), the 8th Chief. His deformity was due to a severe wound between his shoulders received in a battle with the MacDonalds. As well as building the *Fairy Tower* at *Dunvegan*, he re-built St Clement's Church at *Rodel* in 1528 and had a very elaborate tomb prepared for his own burial on the south side of the choir. His tomb is regarded by Historic Scotland as 'the finest ensemble of late medieval sculpture to survive in the isles'. He was the first of several MacLeod Chiefs to be buried at St Clement's. This Chief was perhaps the clan's greatest sponsor of the Arts, giving land rent-free to bards and musicians. It was under his leadership that the first of the MacCrimmon came to prominence and received the lands of *Borreraig*, across *Loch Dunvegan* from the Castle, on which to institute the great piping college. These lands remained in the family until 1770 for the annual rental of *'a penny and a pibroch'*.

Alastair Crotach's diplomatic skills and intrigue brought him favour with King James IV, who granted him charters for his lands, and for *Trotternish* which was then occupied by Clan MacDonald!

At the King's Court in Edinburgh, the confidence and culture of this seemingly illiterate and handicapped Highlander provoked jealousy among the noble Lords. During one lavish meal at the King's Table they commented, *"Surely, MacLeod, you will never have seen such a display of food and wine! You will never have been entertained as you have been tonight! No chandeliers grace your halls!"* Unperturbed by their comments Alexander acknowledged that the Royal Court did provide all creature comforts but that he could produce finer. He duly invited all the company to attend at *Dunvegan* to enjoy the proof. Some months later the Lowland nobility arrived with pomp and ceremony in MacLeod country and were taken at dusk to the top of *Healabhal Mhor*. As darkness fell, the hilltop was circled by clansmen with flaming torches. The finest wines were brought out and served by a retinue of footmen. Salmon and shellfish provided a taste from the sea, venison from the deer forest, beef and lamb from his folds and bread from his mills. Toasts were drunk with the native whisky and the bards and pipers entertained beneath the magnificent candelabra of the stars. The minds of the doubters were put at rest and even the privileged southerners had to agree that the Chief of MacLeod had the most sumptuous fare of all. These two, flat topped hills, *Healabhal Mhor* and *Healabhal Bheag* have ever since been know as *MacLeod's Tables*.

As we turn south to return to the Castle and the village of *Dunvegan*, our view is dominated by the *Tables* until the magnificent *Cuillins* begin to appear on the horizon.

In summer *Dunvegan* is a busy little village and boasts a museum dedicated to the history of the acknowledged world's largest true giant (7ft 10in), Angus Mòr MacAskill. Also, the Guinness Book of World Records lists Angus as the strongest man that ever lived and the man having the largest chest measurements of any non-obese person (80 inches).

Angus was born in 1825 on the *Isle of Berneray* in the *Sound of Harris* and, like so many others, emigrated to Cape Breton in his youth. As a child, his growth was not exceptional, but in adolescence he began to grow very rapidly, but in normal proportion. Aged 20, he was 7ft 4in, his weight 41st 7lb, with shoulder width 44in, his hand 12in long and the palm 8in wide. He wore boots 19in long! Not surprising that he was called *Gille Mor,* translated Big Boy!

There are many tales of Giant MacAskill's feats of strength. He could jog down the street in Englishtown with a 300lb barrel of pork under each arm and was known to lift a 2800lb ship's anchor to shoulder height. Inevitably he was lured into show business and appeared in Barnum's Circus alongside General Tom Thumb.

There are no indications that his parents or any of his forebears were particularly large or strong. His ancestors, the MacAskills of Skye, were the coast watchers for Clan MacLeod and more than once were able to give early warning of the approach of the enemy.

As we come around *Kinloch* at the head of *Loch Dunvegan,* we are reminded that it was here at *Tobar nam Maor* that one of the three Pictish symbol stones found in Skye was first discovered. This stone is now one of the treasures of the Castle. Skye was part of the kingdom of the Picts until 670AD but there is a dispute as to whether the symbols are Christian or Pagan. All three stones have the "crescent and V-rod" and part of the "double disc and Z-rod" symbols. As to what they mean, no key has yet been found.

Meanwhile our journey continues in the direction of *Glendale*, noted for its Big Men, not necessarily in size or strength, more for their intellect and bravery during the Crofting Troubles of the 19th century.

"Tha gillean òga tapaidh
An Gleann-Dail ag eirigh suas
'S cuid aca tha deònach
Air an lòn thoirt thar a' chuan
Ach eisdibh ris an òran
Rinn MacLeòid a chuir air chuairt
'S bi cuimhn' agaibh an còmhnaidh air
'Nuair sheolas sibh a Chluaidh."

"There are hardy young lads
Being brought up in Glendale
And some of them are keen
To make their living on the seas.
But listen to this song
That MacLeod has made and spread
And you will always remember it

When you sail from the Clyde."

Iain (Dubh) MacLeod

CHAPTER 7
Duirinish of the Big Men

As we round *Kinloch*, passing the church glebe, we cross the *River Osdale* (east valley) and pass by *Dun Osdale* on our left. It was at *Dun Osdale* that *'The Scotsman'* Newspaper was burned in effigy for its lack of support for 'The Crofters' Cause' in the 1880s. The place is called *Uaigh an t-Albannaich* ('The Scotsman's' grave). Also at *Osdale* the site of a standing stone has been called the Water Horse's grave listed by the Royal Commission on Ancient and Historical Monuments. The tale goes that a ploughman killed the creature with a red-hot ploughshare.

Our drive takes us up the opposite side of *Loch Dunvegan* from the Castle. The fertile lands of *Uiginish Farm* sit across the water from *Dunvegan* Village and provide views to the *Colbost* islands in a north westerly direction and the islands of *Loch Bracadale* to the south. It was here at *Uiginish Farm* that Frances Tolmie was born in 1840. She was a prolific collector of Gaelic songs, writing down both tunes and lyrics as she heard them. Her collection includes many traditional work songs, cradle lullabies milking songs, grinding songs and tweed-waulking songs. She also helped Neil MacLeod prepare the *'Gesto Collection of Bagpipe Music'* for publication. My great great-granduncle, William Sutherland, was tutor to the family of the tacksman, John Tolmie. We doubt that he tutored little Frances, as her father died in 1845, but the Census of 1841 records, both his presence and that of Frances, at the farmhouse. She and her mother, who was a MacAskill, moved back to her home district of *Minginish* but returned to the Manse of *Bracadale* when Frances' brother, Rev John William Tolmie, became minister there from 1856 to 1863. She died at *Eabost* in 1926.

We pass the township of *Skinidin* (dun of the withered grass) and arrive at *Colbost*. *Colbost* means cold steading but here, at the internationally acclaimed *Three Chimneys Restaurant,* the welcome is warm and the magnificently prepared food rivals *Alistair Crotach's* feast on *MacLeod's Table*. It is not unusual to see guests arrive here for lunch or dinner by helicopter and, no doubt, the feast of scenery as they fly in will stimulate the taste buds. In common with the 16th century feast, the food served here is local produce, nowadays from the crofts, shellfish farms and fisheries around the island. Until fairly recently, the Tourist Industry had failed to take advantage of Skye's superb quality food but, thanks to the efforts of chefs like Shirley Spear, Lady Claire MacDonald, Neil MacNeil and John Kelly, eating out on Skye can, once again, be memorable for all the right reasons.

Dr Johnson said of Skye dining tables, *"I did not observe that the common greens were wanting, and suppose, that by advantageous exposition, they can raise all the more hardy esculent plants. Of vegetable fragrance or beauty they are not yet studious. Few vows are made to Flora in the Hebrides! They have not only eels but pork and bacon in abhorrence, and accordingly I never saw a hog in the Hebrides, except one at Dunvegan."*

Colbost also boasts a thatched croft museum which depicts family life in the 19th century and also an illicit whisky still which is regularly checked by excise officers lest it be brought back into use.

At *Colbost* we bear right and travel through *Totaig* to drop down to *Husabost*. *Husabost House,* built close to the seashore, is still in the possession of the Martin family since it was purchased and extended by Dr. Nicol Martin in 1840. The doctor had lived and worked abroad for much of his life, principally in Demerara in the West Indies. He died aged 84 in 1885 and was the subject of one of Mairi Mhòr's laments. The estate of *Husabost* and *North Glendale* had previously been owned by the Nicolson family. Sheriff Alexander Nicolson born 1827, known as *Alick Husabost* was a famous son of Skye. A brilliant Gaelic scholar, he first began to study for the ministry but then took up a career in journalism before taking up law. Called to the Scottish Bar in 1872 he then became a Sheriff Substitute. He was a lover of his native island and its scenery and was first to climb Skye's highest peak which has been named after him, *Sgurr Alasdair*. Nicolson's articles about Skye in the magazine *'Good Words'* began to attract late 19th century tourists to Skye. Several of his poems, in praise of his beloved island, have become well known.

Skye
My heart is yearning for thee, O Skye!
Dearest of islands!
There first the sunshine gladdened my eye.
On the sea sparkling;
There doth the dust of dear ones lie,
In the old graveyard.

The Isle of Skye
Jerusalem, Athens and Rome,

I would see then before I die,
But I'd rather not see any one of the three
Than be exiled forever from Skye!

Husabost House continues to be important for young bagpipers. My daughter Margaret, as a pupil at Portree High School, competed on several occasions at the annual event which included a visit to the MacCrimmon Cairn at *Borreraig* where the annual rent of *'a penny and a pìobaireachd'* was paid to the Martin landowners. During the March, Strathspey and Reel competition it is customary for the player to march in time to the first tune. The floors of the old house are on such a slope that she felt that the difference between uphill and downhill affected her timing!

The origin of the bagpipes is lost in the mists of the past, but the instrument came into prominence, in peace and war, during the early 16th century. From this time to the present, the Great Highland Bagpipes have consisted of a mouthpiece, a chanter and three drones attached to the bag. One of the famous bards of Clan MacDonald, *Niall Mòr MacMhuirich,* composed a poem 'The History of the Descent of the Bagpipes from the Earliest Times' which gives an idea of the development of the instrument from the time when there were no drones.

"A' cheud mhàla nach robh binn,
Thainig bho thùs na Dilinn.

"The first bagpipe, that was not sweet,
Came from the beginning of the Flood.

Cha robh 'nuair sin anns a' phiob,
Ach sionnsair, agus aon liop,
Agus maide, chumadh nam fonn,

In the pipe there was only,
The chanter and one mouthpiece,
With a rod that harmonised with the
music,

Do 'm b' ainm an sumaire.

And was called the drone.

Tamull dhaibh na dheidh sin
Do fhuair as-innleachd innleachd,
Agus chinnich na tri chroinn innt',
Fear dhiubh fada, leobhar, garbh,
Ri durdan reamhar ro shearbh."

Some time thereafter
This crude artifice led to an invention,
And three drones developed,
One of them long clumsy and rough,
Droning coarsely and harsh."

The oldest, existing set of pipes has a date of 1409 associated with it. This has two drones only, jointed on one stock. No bass drone is present.

This area of Skye is of course the World's home of bagpipe music. The great MacCrimmon family once lived at *Galtrigill* but were also granted lands at *Borreraig* on which was founded their famous Piping College. Pipers from all the great clans, both in Scotland and Ireland, were sent by their chiefs to learn from the great masters.

Like the history of the pipes themselves, there is some debate as to where the MacCrimmon family originated. Some claim that the first piper was brought to Skye by a MacLeod Chief who heard his skilled playing while on campaign in Cremona in Italy. This seems very unlikely and the tale probably originated from an attempt to reconcile the surname Mac – Crimmon, as Son of Cremona, and/or, that the first know piping exponent in the family was named *Iain Odhar* (dun coloured John, from his sallow complexion). Others aver that the name was from the Irish, *Crimthan* (wolf) and this may well be so. It is acknowledged that the surname was known in Harris in the 13th century when Paul Balkeson was 'Sheriff of the Isles'. Whether there were pipers in the family before the early 16th century *Iain Odhar MacCrimmon*, is also quite likely. *Iain Odhar* flourished in the time of the great Chief *Alasdair Crotach* and probably provided the entertainment at the great Table Feast!

The MacArthur pipers to Clan MacDonald and the great John MacKay *(Am Pìobaire Dall)* (The Blind Piper) of Gairloch, all studied under the MacCrimmon tutors at *Borreraig* and old enmities were forgotten so long as music was being learned.

"Thig crioch air an t-saoghal,   *"The World will end,*
Ach mairidh gaol is ceòl."   *But love and music will endure."*

The MacCrimmon tuition was based on a system of notation called *canntaireachd* or vocalising. The desired notes were represented by vowel sounds, so that the tune and rhythm could be learned and remembered more easily. The simpler *Ceol Beag* Jigs, Reels, Airs, Strathspeys and Marches were mastered by the pupils, but greater emphasis was placed on learning the classical music, *Ceol Mòr* or *Pìobaireachd*. Most of the greatest *pìobaireachd* were composed by the MacCrimmons.

Each *pìobaireachd* consists of a theme first stated in a slow movement called the ground or in Gaelic the **ùrlar**. The **siubhal** which follows contains a number of singling and doubling variations with Gaelic names *lemluath*, *taorluath* and *crunluath*, each with rapid offsets called *breabach*. To finish off, the tune returns to a repetition of the original ground.

Of the well known tunes, one might expect *Iain Odhar's* 'MacCrimmon's Sweetheart', to praise his wife or his lover, but this piper's sweetheart was the bag of his pipes! Donald *Mòr* MacCrimmon composed 'MacLeod's Welcome' in 1601 and the great *Pàdruig Mòr* was perhaps the best and most prolific MacCrimmon composer. One of his most famous tunes is, 'I gave a Kiss to the King's Hand', following his meeting with King Charles II prior to his crowning at Scone in 1651.

    Pàdruig Mòr was succeeded by *Pàdruig Og*, then Malcolm, then *Iain Dubh*. Donald *Bàn* MacCrimmon set off from Dunvegan in 1746, knowing that he would never return. He was the only person killed at the *Rout of Moy*.

Cha Till MacCruimein
"Dh' iadh ceò nan stùc mu aodann Chuilinn,
Is sheinn a' bhean-shìth a torman mulaid;
Tha sùilean gorm ciùin 's an Dùn a' sileadh
O'n thriall thu uainn 's nach till thu tuilleadh.

Cha till, Cha till, Cha till, MacCruimein,
An cogadh no'n sìth cha till e tuilleadh;
Le airgoid no nì cha till MacCruimein,
Cha till e gu bràth gu là na cruinne!"

MacCrimmon's Lament
"Round Cuillin' peaks the mist is sailing,
The banshee croons her note of wailing,
Mild blue eyes with sorrow are streaming
For him that shall never return, MacCrimmon.

No more, no more, no more forever,
In war or peace, shall return MacCrimmon;
No more, no more, no more forever,
Shall silver or love bring back MacCrimmon."

As the MacLeod Chiefs became anglified they lost interest in their bards, pipers and harpists, and Norman the 22nd Chief, took away half of the MacCrimmons' *Borreraig* Farm for his own use.

It might be expected that so famous a family of skilled musicians would tend to attract the attention of the *sgeulaiche* (teller of tales or legends). There are many legends of how the family might have got their prowess, and perhaps the best concerns the 'Silver Chanter of the Fairy Woman', *('Sionnsair Airgoid na Mna Sìthe')*.

Alasdair Crotach had invited many of the nobility to *Dunvegan* for a competition to choose the most skilled piper. The MacLeod Chief was sure that his resident piper would out-perform the best of the MacArthurs and the MacIntyres and so had placed a large wager on him. In the event, the champion, through illness or alcohol (the curse of the piper!), was unable to 'blow up the bag'. The young MacCrimmon apprentice was called and informed that he must take his place and, of the pressure he was under! In fear and trepidation he went out on the battlements to tune his instrument. His fingers trembled so much that he could not play a note. Just then, a little green fairy appeared and offered to help. She gave him a chanter of solid silver, but warned him that, no matter what went wrong in life, neither he, nor his successors, must ever blame the chanter for any misfortune. When his turn came to play, the competition was easily won and everyone praised both young MacCrimmon and his sponsor. MacLeod won his wager and the lad returned to *Borreraig*, where he passed on his new-found skills to his family and founded the college. Many years later, while the MacLeod Chief of the time was sailing across to Harris, his MacCrimmon piper was in the bow of the galley playing a joyful tune when his cold fingers slipped so that his pipes emitted a shriek. In frustration he cursed the silver chanter. Immediately the chanter jumped out of the bagpipe and sunk to the bottom of the Minch, never to be seen again. From that day forth, the MacCrimmons lost, and never regained, their skills!

Nowadays, at the August Isle of Skye Games, the winner of the previous year's *Pìobaireachd* competition is invited to play, along with other top pipers, at *Dunvegan Castle* for the prestigious 'Silver Chanter Trophy'. A short-list of tunes is chosen and each piper is given, on the night, the name of the one he is expected to play to World Class standard. This, of course, means that s/he must know all of the tunes on the list and be prepared to play any! At the MacCrimmon College, a master was expected to remember one hundred and ninety five *pìobaireachd*! No wonder seven years was considered the minimum course length at *Borreraig*.

Beyond *Borreraig* is the present day township of *Galtrigill*. There are only a few houses here but, beyond the roadend can be seen the ruins of considerably more dwellings. Like many places in the Highlands, the absence of suitable roads to the farthest townships made life more difficult. We are told that because their peat bogs were considerably below the level of the houses, it became too difficult to haul, fuel and fertiliser (seaweed) up to the crofts.

It's here at *Galtrigill* that we find 'The Manners Stone'. Local guide books insist that by sitting on it, or walking around it three times, you will improve your manners. One locally produced leaflet suggests that the sitting position will only prove effective if "nothing is worn 'twixt cheek and stone". I think it unlikely in this connection however, that the English word 'Manners' would be used by a Gaelic speaking community. Alasdair Alpin MacGregor tells that *Glendale* folk had informed him that in olden times "the sheriff or judge sat here to administer the law". This is a more likely scenario. Perhaps the original name was *'Clach Manadh'* (the stone of prophecy or enchantment), or *'Clach Mhanach'* (the Monk's stone)?

But then of course *'manachan'* does mean buttock!!!

Galtrigill is the starting point for a two mile walk to the cliffs of *Dunvegan Head*. Aiming for the highest point at *Biod an Athair* (Cliff of the Sky), you will be 1000feet above the sea with the most magnificent views in all directions. From the trig point, with the *Cuillin* and *MacLeod's Tables* behind you, *Neist point* and its lighthouse will be on your left, the *Western Isles* ahead and the *Vaternish Wing* to your right. If you then walk towards *Dunvegan Head* and return to your starting point you will have a fine view of the Natural Arch and some bee-hive dwellings.

It was from *Biod an Athair* that another famous MacCrimmon warned of an attack on MacLeod lands by the MacDonalds. *Fionnlaidh na Plaide Baine* (Finlay of the White Plaid) was said to have given three mighty shouts from the summit, which were heard by the watchman at the Castle seven miles away! It was this Finlay who deflated the 'Bullies' who acted as the bodyguard for Norman MacLeod the 12th Chief. Having killed his best cow, they had ordered Finlay's wife to cook the best parts of it for themselves. When the man of the house returned home from rock fishing, he set about all twelve of them with a flail until they were beaten into submission. His wife then tied each one with fishing twine by the ankles, wrists and neck *(ceangal nan coig caol)* while Finlay stood over them. He then transported them one by one to his boat and rowed them across the loch to the Castle. Acknowledging the strength and tenacity of Finlay, the Chief dismissed his twelve bodyguards and replaced them with this one strongman!

Back at *Galtrigill* we remember another famous son of this township. Donald MacLeod of *Galtrigill*, an inter-island merchant by trade, became famous as a guide to Bonnie Prince Charlie. Unlike his vacillating Chief, Donald made acquaintance with the Jacobites while collecting a wagon-load of meal at Inverness and made his loyalty clear. Because of his local knowledge he was given the task of bringing £380 in gold from *Barra* to the mainland for use in the campaign. This was accomplished successfully and the money was hidden at *Moidart*. By this time the Prince had been defeated at *Culloden* and, when he arrived at *Loch nan Uamh,* it was Donald who navigated him safely throughout his two months of travel in the *Western Isles*. After the Prince had made his way back to Skye in the charge of Flora MacDonald, Donald was betrayed and captured in *Benbecula*. As a prisoner for ten long months aboard the government ship *'Furnace'* Donald suffered considerably but said of his captors, *"God forgive them. We are sure that we would not treat them as they have treated us. We would show them the difference between a good and a bad cause."* When taunted that he could easily have claimed the £30,000 bounty money on the Prince's head, this honest and loyal man said, *"This conscience of mine would have got up upon me and that money would not have kept it down! I would not allow a hair of his body to be touched if I could help it."* He was finally released on 10ᵗʰ July 1747 but, as a result of his cruel treatment he died on 8ᵗʰ September 1749. Alexander Nicolson in his *'History of Skye'* says, *"His name will be remembered with pardonable pride so long as loyalty, fortitude and a disinterested regard for those in distress awaken the admiration of mankind, for his was a noble role!"*

In order to make progress toward the next stage of our trip we must drive back from *Galtrigill* via *Borreraig* to the small township of *Uig* or *Borreraig Parks* where there is a new Piping Museum, and then turn right to make our way over the ridge into *Glendale*. The local community website tells us that there are forty two *Glendales* in the World, must of them in the USA, but Skye's *Glendale* is the oldest, first settled between 800 and 1000AD. The name, of course, is a Gaelic/Norse combination word meaning 'valley valley'. Like New York, 'it's so good they named it twice'!

We enter the glen at the township of *Feriniquaire* or *Ferinaquarrie* (the land of Godfrey's son). It's said that this area had been promised to a son of the MacDonald Chief prior to a clan raid on this part of MacLeod territory in 1492. The MacDonalds had 'counted their chickens before they were hatched', however, as they were severely defeated at the *Battle of Glendale* in that year, and were forced to abandon their plans. Some say that this was the battle where the MacLeod Chief, *Alasdair Crotach*, received the wound which caused his deformity and that his wife had brought the Fairy Flag to the battle-field.

Down by the *Hamara River* there is little to be seen of the ancient St Comgan's Church (*Kilchoan*) and it's equally ancient graveyard, the burial place of the Danish Prince Tiel. This hero, a king's son, had been killed in a sea-battle and was taken ashore by his warriors at *Loch a' Chuain* (Loch of the Ocean). From that time the Loch was given its new name *Loch Pooltiel*. Tradition tells that a twisted elder tree (still visible) grows from the Prince's grave and must never be cut or pruned. But Tiel is not the only hero buried here. John MacPherson (1845 - 1924) 'the Glendale Martyr' lies in St. Comgan's. Throughout the poetry of Dr Sorley MacLean there is repeated reference to this hero who stood up to the cruel treatment and clearing of his people.

"*Ach Diùirinis nan criosan creige*
Far na chaisgeadh sgreamh nan eilean,
Far an tug na Dalaich breaban
Gu caistealan móra leagail."
....

"But Duirinish with its belts of rock,
Where the disgust of the islands was checked,
Where the Glendale men first kicked
To bring down big castles."
....

"*Thàinig Iain, an said,*
A Cille-Chòmhghain shìos sa Ghleann;
Cha deachaidh aoibhneas-san am miad
Ag éisdeachd a' ghoileim a bha ann."

"Then came John, man of men,
From St Comgan's down in the Glen;
His mirth did not increase
Listening to that gabbling."

From *'The New York Times'* of 15th November 1886 we read;
> *"John MacPherson, who is known as the 'Glendale Martyr', and the Rev Mr. Donald MacCallum have been arrested in the Isle of Skye on the charge of inciting violence. Mr. MacCallum, as Chairman, advised a meeting of crofters to resist the removal of cattle. Mr. MacPherson also spoke at the meeting, giving the crofters similar advice."*

In 1852 Sir John MacPherson MacLeod purchased the 20,000 acre *Glendale Estate* from the trustees of MacLeod of MacLeod. He died, 29 years later, in 1881, having visited the area only **once!!** The estate was then left to his 24 year old nephew, the ornithologist Rev Hugh MacPherson who was a minister in Carlisle. He loved Skye but only spent holidays at Hamara Lodge. Did these landowners know anything of the conditions of their tenants and/or did they care? Perhaps not, but they certainly should have done. Management of the estate was in the hands of a factor, Donald MacDonald of *'Tormore'*. By all accounts, his regime was tyrannical. The crofters were not allowed to keep a dog, cut down a tree, collect driftwood, or allow their cattle on their traditional grazings and were required to make themselves available for estate work at the sound of the tacksman's horn. In May 1882, following the very positive publicity that the arrest of the *Braes* crofters had engendered, the *Glendale* men took courage and released their cattle onto the grazings at *Waterstein*. Several court orders for their removal were ignored. In November, when one of the estate shepherds tried to remove the cattle, he was assaulted by their owners.

"An sluagh bha cho càirdeil,	"The people who were so friendly,
Cho suairc', is cho bàidheil,	So civil and so warm,
Rinn uachdarain stràiceil	Haughty landlords
Am fàsgadh ro threann,	Squeezed them too tightly,
Tha saors' air am fàgail,	They are bereft of their freedom,
Tha 'n raointean 'nam fàsaich',	And their fields are a wilderness,
'S tha caoraich an àite	And the sheep have the place
Nan àrmunn 's a' ghleann."	Of the heroes of the glen."

Neil MacLeod

By Christmas, warrants were issued for the arrest of twenty crofters and four new policemen were stationed in the area but their postings were short-lived, as locals made clear that their presence was not welcome. The response of the Government, clearly very concerned at yet more trouble in Skye, was to send the gunboats 'Jackal' and 'Sea Horse' to *Loch Pooltiel* to intimidate the people, while fully armed marines and policemen accompanied the notorious Sheriff Ivory on a march over the ridge from *Colbost*. The Naval Officers were nonplussed to discover the loyal crofters flying Union Flags and welcoming them with open arms. The Government emissary met with a group of Skye ministers at the *Glendale* Free Church to thresh out a compromise; a Royal Commission would be set up (the usual Government delaying tactic), but a token three men, John MacPherson, Donald MacLeod and John Morrison would stand trial. They became known as the 'Glendale Martyrs'. They are commemorated by a memorial cairn on the main road into the Glen where 600 of the local people gathered, unarmed, to 'welcome' the troops with prayers and psalm singing.

At the Court of Session in Edinburgh, all three men were convicted of 'breach of interdict and contempt of court' and were sentenced to two months imprisonment. They returned to Skye as heroes. On 8th May 1883, Lord Napier began taking evidence from crofters around the Highlands. The slogan, *"A tenantry is mightier than a lord"*, *"Is treise tuath na tighearna"*, helped the election of four Land League Members of Parliament from Highlands and Islands constituencies. These were among the first truly working-class MPs. It seems very likely that the conclusions of the Napier Commission would have been buried in obscurity had not the crofters, Land League, MPs and newspapers kept up the pressure on Prime Minister William Gladstone. The Crofters' Struggle was now newsworthy across the World! The further arrest of MacPherson and Rev MacCallum brought matters to a head. Màiri Mhòr said:

"*Chunnaic sinn bristeadh na fàire,*
'*S neòil na tràillealachd air chall,*
An là a sheas MacCaluim làimh rinn
Aig Beul-àtha-nan trì-allt."

"We saw the dawn break, and the
clouds of thralldom flee away, the
day MacCallum stood beside us at
the Fairy Bridge."

The Crofters' Holding Act was passed that year; 1886,
giving security of tenure to crofters, making them immune
from eviction and allowing them to pass on their crofts to
their heirs.

Dr Sorley MacLean clearly thought that Skye, and the
Highlands, owed a considerable debt of gratitude to the radical
orator John MacPherson who was imprisoned several times,
having ignored the advice of colleagues, "Bend the Law but
don't break it!"

On the death of Rev Hugh MacPherson, the *Glendale Estate*
was sold back to MacLeod of MacLeod but in 1903 was
purchased by the Congested Districts Board, in effect, the State.
This body made considerable improvements in the area, giving
work to locals in building roads and piers and in drainage and
stock improvement. In 1911, their function was taken over by
the Board of Agriculture. *Glendale* crofters were the first in
Scotland to take on individual ownership of their crofts and the
estate was administered by a local committee. Until the 1976
Crofters' Reform Act, which gave all crofters the right to
purchase their land, crofters in other parts of the country
remained as tenant farmers. It is very doubtful if this 'right to
buy' has been a good thing as the desire 'to sell off the family
silver' for 'filthy lucre' is a vice not confined to the gentry!
Perhaps this is why *Glendale* now has the dubious distinction
of being referred to as 'Little England'!

Among other 'Big Men' of *Glendale*, who loved 'their patch of
native earth', were Donald MacLeod *(Do'ull nan Oran)*
(Donald of the Songs) and his sons Neil and John. All three were
poets of a very high order. Donald, born in *Pollosgain* in 1787,

had produced an anthology of verse running to some 250 pages by 1811, when he was only twenty-four years of age. His skills in the vocabulary and idiom of the Gaelic language marked him out as a superb storyteller and historian as well as a satirist and humourist. In his poem *'Smeòrach'* (The Song Thrush) he refers to the Norse origin of Clan MacLeod.

"Cha b'i crionach liath no mosgan,
Bho'n a shiolaich treud an fhortainn;
Ach fiodh miath, gun mhiar, gun socadh,
Geal mar ghrian, bho bhian Rìgh Lochluinn."

"It was not from hoary or dead wood
That the fortunate tribe derived
But from healthy timber without knot or water-logging,
A kindred white like the Sun from the lustre of the King of Norway."

Donald had various jobs; collector of road-taxes, fisherman to *Dunvegan Castle* and after his return from a brief sojourn in America, shopkeeper in *Glendale*. His young fiancé died suddenly so he remained unmarried until he came back from the States at the age of sixty. He then married a young lady aged only nineteen and had a family of four sons and six daughters. His sons John and Neil inherited different strains of their father's poetic skills. John *(Iain Dubh)* went to sea and composed witty poems and patriotic songs. Neil's work is better known, particularly his love songs and songs of love for his native island. His collection of poems *Clàrsach nan Doire* had four editions printed in his lifetime.

"Chan 'eil fearann, chan 'eil fonn
Aig mo rìghinn òig;
Ach tha cridhe glan 'n a com
Aig mo rìghinn òig.
Ged a bhiodh ar bothan lom,
Is ar sporran gun bhith trom,
Bhithinn sona ris an tom,
Le mo rìghinn òig."

"Neither farm nor croft
Has my young maiden
But a pure heart
Has my maiden.
Though our hovel should be bare,
And our purse light,
I would be happy in the lea of a mound,
With my young maiden."

"*Thoir dhòmhsa sìth, is gràdh, is gaol,*
Ri taobh nan sruthan tlàth,
Mo bhothan beag fo sgàil nan craobh,
'S mo lios ri taobh na tràigh."

"Give me peace, charity and love,
Beside the gentle streams,
My little cottage under the trees,
And my garden beside the sea."
"Come poverty or riches,

"*Thigeadh bochdainn no bearteas,*
Thigeadh acaid no leòn,
Chaoidh cha sgar iad mo chuimhne
Bho na glinn sin ri m'bheo;
Ged a shiubhlainn gach rioghachd
Is gach tir fo na neòil,
Bidh mo chridhe gu deireadh
Ann an Eilean a' cheò,"

Come grief or wound,
Never will they sever my memory
From these glens where I live;
Though I were to traverse
Every kingdom under the sun,
My heart will be forever
In the Island of the Mist."

Both Donald and Neil are buried at *St Comgan's* but *Iain Dubh's* grave is in Montreal, a fact that was predicted by himself as a young man. He is believed to have had the gift, or curse, of Second Sight.

In some circles Magnus MacLean will be regarded as the greatest of the "Big Men" of *Glendale* because he came to be known as one of Britain's great scientists of the 19th and early 20th century, as well as a distinguished Gaelic scholar.

On coming to Glasgow in 1877 to qualify for the teaching profession he entered the Free Church Training College. After some experience as a teacher in Sutherlandshire, he resumed study at Glasgow University in November, 1881. At his entrance examinations he won the Lorimer Bursary in Mathematics which helped to fund his studies; and soon afterwards he was appointed a "Thomson" experimental scholar in the physical laboratory.

MacLean was selected in 1884 by Lord Kelvin, then Sir William Thomson, as chief assistant in the class of Natural Philosophy. In this post he soon acquired a reputation as a successful lecturer and teacher of science. As a result, in addition to his assistant-professorship, he was appointed by the University Court in 1892, Lecturer on Physics to medical students, and in 1895 Lecturer on Pure and Applied Electricity to the engineering students of the University. During his tenure of office he found time to prosecute original investigations, the results of which he contributed either singly or jointly with Lord Kelvin and others to various learned societies, such as the Philosophical Society of Glasgow, the Royal Societies of London and Edinburgh, and the British Association; and his *alma mater* conferred on him the further degree of D.Sc.. In 1899 Dr MacLean was appointed Professor of Electrical Engineering at Glasgow Technical College, which was later to become Strathclyde University. Here, at least two of his students were to become famous; John Logie Baird, inventor of television, and Lord Reith, 'father of the BBC'. Logie Baird's graduation scroll bears the signature of Professor Magnus MacLean.

He also became the first Celtic Lecturer in the University of Glasgow and his lectures were published in two volumes under the titles *'The Literature of the Celts'* and *'The Literature of the Highlands'*. In 1903 he was a member of the Mosely Education Commission to the United States, and contributed a report and various press articles on the visit.

Magnus became a firm friend as well as colleague of Lord Kelvin and a correspondent of Albert Einstein. It is believed that, although moving in these exalted circles, he continued to provide moral support for his cousin John MacPherson in 'The Crofters' Struggle'.

Visiting the Glen in early summer when it is lush and green is truly a delight. Birdsong is in the air and the scent of wildflowers intoxicates the senses. The primroses and violets of spring are followed by bluebells and ten varieties of wild orchids. How lucky we are to have such lovely places on our island. Even in winter, when the vegetation colours are dull browns and greys, there is interest here when we observe flocks of lapwings gyrating over the croft land, curlews on the moor and golden plovers down by the loch. Perhaps it's the black and white oystercatchers with their brilliant orange beaks and the black guillemots with their bright red legs which help to give some colour to this season and conspire to lift the spirits. The oystercatcher *(gille-brìde or bridean)* (the page of Bride) is said to be named for St Bride who carried one in each hand on arrival in the Western Isles. Their warning cry *"bi glic, bi glic"* means "be wise" or "take care" and mariners regarded it as a warning of approaching storm. If you have time to stay a while, you may spot snipe, sandpipers and rock pipits along the shoreline and mallard, eider duck and red-breasted mergansers on the water. Around the gardens chaffinches, goldfinches and greenfinches are joined by siskins, goldcrests, wrens and tits, while wheatears, stonechats and swallows visit in summer. No wonder Hugh MacPherson could list so many observations.

The townships in the Glen, like so many in Skye, have names, half from Norse and half from Gaelic. *Feriniquaire, Glasphein, Fasach, Lephin* and *Pollosgan* are from Gaelic and *Holmisdale, Hamera, Miolavaig, Borrodale* and *Meanish* from Norse.

A brief stop at *Meanish Pier* gives views up the Glen and out to sea. Of particular interest is the spectacular waterfall which cascades from the slopes of *Ben Ettow*. Nowadays, with our plethora of modern communications, radio, television, internet, e-mail and mobile phone it is easy for us to forget that less than fifty years ago the people of the Highlands were very dependant on the 'steamer' as a means of contact with the outside world. The local people and their visitors came and went by boat as it was a much more pleasant journey than to endure the rough roads. For this reason *Meanish Pier* was very important to the people of the Glen over the years. It was to the pier that supplies came on cargo boats from Glasgow, passenger ships called and cattle from the Uists were transported here to begin their long walk to the trysts at Falkirk and Crieff. Before roads assumed their present importance, sea travel was much more common for Skye's inhabitants. Ian Anderson, in his travel book *'To Introduce the Hebrides'*, recalled his arrival in *Loch Poolteil* in the early 1900s. *"Shortly before midnight the Hebrides glided alongside*

Poolteil Pier and really I almost felt as if I had suddenly entered into the centre of a village 'social'. At the corner of the pier stood the Pier Master swinging his oil lantern for the ship's guidance to assist it in berthing. The open-fronted shed on the pier was filled with people of both sexes and all ages, from all parts of the surrounding district, and all actively engaged in conversation under the feeble yellow rays of the oil lamp illuminating the shed. It was an animated scene, and the quick sound of the Gaelic and shrill laughter of the children and the soft cadence of the Highlanders' English, lent a warmth of friendliness to the gathering. The arrival of the Hebrides broke up this company and the business of assisting with the unloading, and the claiming of respective articles of merchandise was set to. This was seemingly an event and it appeared that all came to the pier whether for goods or not. The pier was the meeting-place for this outlying community. No sooner was the cargo unloaded than the people began to drift away in twos and threes, and as our ropes were drawn aboard, even the man with the lamp of guidance had disappeared."

On those sea lochs around Skye where there were no piers or easily accessible landing-places, the little puffers which carried fuel and general cargo, would glide in on the high tide. Because of their unique construction they could gently settle on the flat sea-bed as the tide went out. The cargo was soon off-loaded by winch or donkey-crane into horse-and-cart or light motor lorry. This procedure was common and provided a much appreciated life-line into the second half of the twentieth century. The puffers *Glencloy, Dawnlight, Polarlight* were among the last to transport cargo to Skye.

Nowadays it's pleasure boats and sea-angling boats which use the pier and slipway at *Meanish*. *Oisgill* and *Moonen* Bays are ideal for angling, and lots of big fish are there for the taking, but the pleasure of observing porpoises, dolphins, as well as minke whales, basking sharks and, occasionally, killer whales (orca), far out weighs the thrill of fishing; as far as most of our visitors are concerned.

The journey upwards through *Miolavaig* to *Waterstein* takes us by *Druim nan Sgarbh* (cormorant's ridge), which was perhaps named because the green cormorants and their smaller cousins, the shags, take a short cut over the hill from *Moonen Bay* (named after an Ossianic hero called Munan) to the relatively more sheltered waters of *Loch Pooltiel*. On the skerries all around the coast, these birds can be seen with wings outstretched drying their feathers in the wind and sun. Their appearance in this pose can be rather spooky! They look like gryphons from another age. Unlike all other diving birds, they do not have waterproofing oil on their wing feathers and so require drying off when they resurface. Rather than this being a disadvantage, wet down helps to decrease buoyancy. Cormorants are also able to alter the specific gravity of their bodies at will, by letting out air from their lungs and air sacs. When alarmed they can sink deeper in the water so that only the neck appears above the surface like a periscope.

The township of *Waterstein* is dominated by *Loch Mòr* where whooper swans and several species of passage migrant geese are often seen. Beyond the township the local Council have bowed to the pressure of tourist vehicles and lined out a car park. This is, of course a much visited spot. *Neist Point* or *Rubha na h-Eist* (Stallion Point), and the high cliff is called *An t-Aigeach* (another word for stallion), can now be regarded as the furthest point west on the British mainland! At least there is a good argument for this, since Skye now has its bridge!

From the car park there is a delightful one mile walk to the lighthouse, built in 1909 at a cost of £4350 by David Stevenson. Prior to that time, this coastline was notorious for the number of ships wrecked on the cliffs and skerries. In 1900 a Dutch vessel went aground in fog at the *Eist*. Shortly afterwards another ship foundered on a sunken rock, known as 'The Gruagach' in Oisgill Bay. These events prompted the building of this welcome navigation aid.

More recently the film 'Breaking the Waves' starring Emily Lloyd was shot here and for several years, a cemetery, which had been constructed as part of the film set was allowed to remain to litter the landscape. From a distance, many visitors thought it was real!

Like all lighthouses around the British coast this one is now automatic (it was manned until 1989) and the out-buildings have been converted for self-catering. They are particularly popular at Christmas and New Year. Just the spot to get away from it all, but quite an experience in a southwesterly winter storm!

From late April until the end of September, with June/July being the peak months, this is one of the best places in the British Isles for spotting minke whales and basking sharks, but there have been no recent sightings of little people in Fairy Bay (*Camus nan Sìthean*).

Returning from *Waterstein* we turn right at *Borrodale* and drive five miles along the lonely road to *Ramasaig*, looking out across the cliffs to the Atlantic. There are only a couple of houses at *Ramasaig* (N. *hrafns-vik*, Raven's Bay) but plenty of evidence that there was once a significant population here. Derek Cooper tells us that *Ramasaig* was reputed to be the home of *Black Bess*, the fastest mare ever bred in Skye. *"In November 1892 Magnus Murcheson, mounted on Black Bess, left Portree Post Office at 8 in the morning and arrived in Glendale, 30 miles away, at 12.45. Black Bess served with the Lovat Scouts and died in Ramasaig at the advanced age of 32."*

This vast area of moorland was made into a large sheep farm in the early 19th century and there are still large flocks of cheviot sheep on the hill. The tarred road stops at *Ramasaig* but, for the intrepid, there is a ten mile track to *Orbost* which follows the *Lòn Bàn* to *Lorgill* and then by the coast via *Cnoc Fuar*, *Glen Dibidal*, *Glen Ollisdal* and *Glen Lorgasdal* to the *MacLeod's Maidens*. As a schoolboy I walked this route in reverse from *Orbost* to *Ramasaig* with the High School Field Club. The views are truly stunning and, because the weather was perfect, we were not concerned about the remoteness. It would be a very different matter however if the weather was inclement, as there is now no human habitation on this whole route. About half a mile from the track, up *Glen Ollisdale,* there is a hut maintained by the Mountain Bothies Association which has sheltered many a wet and windswept adventurer.

Lorgill once had a thriving community of ten families and it is still a very beautiful place but one day in July 1830 a small party consisting of the factor, the sheriff officer, four policemen and the minister arrived with a written notice which read:

"To all the crofters in Lorgill.

Take notice that you are hereby duly warned that you all be ready to leave Lorgill at twelve o'clock on the 4th August next with all your baggage but no stock and proceed to Loch Snizort, where you will board the ship Midlothian (Captain Morrison) that will take you to Nova Scotia, where you are to receive a free grant of land from Her Majesty's Government. Take further notice that any crofter disobeying this order will be immediately arrested and taken to prison. All persons over seventy years of age and who have no relatives to look after them will be taken care of in the County Poorhouse. This order is final and no appeal to the Government will be considered.

God Save the Queen."

On the appointed day the whole community obeyed the order and, after laying flowers on the graves of their loved ones, they sang the 100th Psalm and trudged away with much weeping. Their house roofs were fired by the factor to prevent their return. It is recorded that the *Lorgill* people were never again heard of in Skye. Did they arrive in Nova Scotia? Was the ship lost at sea?

"Tha na fàrdaichean 'n am fàsach
Far an d'araicheadh na seòid,
Far'm bu chridheil fuaim n gàire
Far'm bu chàirdeil iad mu'n bhòrd
Far am faigheadh coigreach bàigh
Agus ànrach bochd a lòn
Ach chàn fhaigh iad sin 'san àm so
Anns a' ghleann 's an robh mi òg."

"The dwellings are desolate
Where warriors were reared,
Where hearty was the sound of their laughter,
Where they were hospitable round the table,
Where the alien could find kindness
And the poor stranger, food,
But they will not get that now,
In the glen where I was young."

Neil MacLeod.

The *Macleod's Maidens* are three sea stacks which are situated off *Idrigill Point* at the entrance to *Loch Bracadale*. Sir Walter Scott called these rocks "The Choosers of the Slain" and "Riders of the Storm", a reference to the last of the Valkyries who fled at the coming of Christianity to *Durinish*.

Many ships have perished here. John the 4th Chief of MacLeod was about to embark for *Dunvegan* from Harris when he was stabbed to death. His wife and two daughters, already in the galley, drifted out to sea without oarsmen or sail. They were shipwrecked off *Idrigill Point*. Perhaps they are the *Maidens of MacLeod*?

But, as no vehicles can travel to *Orbost* by this route, we must backtrack to *Borrodale*. At *Borrodale* School the pupils can feed and learn about the Highland cattle, one of which is of the original black type. It is interesting to see that a number of crofters keep Hebridean sheep which are also black. Their wool is prized for spinning and weaving.

We go back through *Glendale*, but this time on the main road down to the former *Colbost* School which is now the home of 'Skye Silver', where quality jewellery is produced. We rejoin our outward route and continue to the *River Osdale* where we turn off right to *Orbost*. *Orbost House* was purchased by Otta Swire and her husband from the executry of her late uncle. It had been the home of her maternal grandparents. Here on *Loch Bharcasaig* we have entered one of the nooks of *"many-nooked Loch Bracadale"*, as Dr. Sorley MacLean describes it.

CHAPTER 8

Bracadale
Of Sheep and Shepherds

The fairly wide entrance to *Loch Bracadale* lies between *Idrigill Point* and *Rubha nan Clach*, but it then broadens out further to give access to many long sea lochs which penetrate Skye. Dr Sorley MacLean describes it as, *"Loch Bhràcadail ioma-chùilteach"*, "many-nooked Loch Bracadale". The Vikings called it *Vestrafjord* or *Wester Fjord* and it was here in 1263 that King Haakon's Norse fleet rested to lick their wounds following their defeat by Alexander III at the Battle of Largs.

When Thomas Pennant visited Skye in 1772 he saw the potential for *Loch Bracadale*. *"This seems to me,"* he said, *"the fittest place in the island for the forming of a Town. The harbour is unspeakably secure. It is the Milford Haven of these parts; it opens at its mouth to the best part of the sea."*

There are several significant islands in *Loch Bracadale*. Some, like *Wiay*, *Oronsay*, *Harlosh* and *Tarner*, were inhabited until the 19th century, but are now of use only for sheep grazing. A 17th century writer tells us that on these islands redcurrants grew wild and in abundance.

In the year 1891 a ship the 'Yemasse', carrying a cargo of crockery, bound for the Baltic was wrecked near *Bharcasaig* in *Loch Bracadale*. There was no loss of life and the seafarers were given hospitality at *Orbost House*. In my grandparents' house *'Craiglea'* at *Struan* there is a large oak beam which is reputed to have come from a ship wrecked in *Loch Bracadale*. Was this the ship? Wrecks were common beyond *Idrigill Point* but not so in the more sheltered waters of the Loch! Otta Swire however, records that the sand in *Bharcasaig Bay* was once white but turned black in one night of storm!

Our journey continues around the many townships along the shores of this delightful part of Skye. *Greep* on *Loch na Faolinn* was, in the first half of the 20th century, the home of the Campbell family of superb Gaelic singers, and the next generation continues to please audiences with their musical accomplishments. The Campbells were particularly well known for the traditional *'port-a-beul'* or 'mouth music' which puts words to the rhythmic Celtic jigs and reels and *'orain luaidh'*, songs sung to accompany the waulking, or shrinking, of the tweed. Pennant says *"the subjects of these songs are sometimes of love, sometimes panegyric, and often a rehearsal of the deeds of the ancient heroes, but all the tunes slow and melancholy."*

Roag and *Pool Roag* were anchorages for the *birlinn* or galleys of Clan MacLeod and were often used by visiting clan chiefs. Only a short distance by land from *Dunvegan Castle*, perhaps it was easier to put back to sea from here, than to sail out of the narrower *Loch Follart*! Why the Norse gave it this name, *Roag*, 'the noisy place' is difficult to imagine as nowadays it is a haven of peace!

Keeping to the by-roads we go by *Vatten* to *Harlosh* where the 5th Chief of MacLeod, *Uilleam Cléireach*, brought the booty from raids on the mainland estates belonging to Fraser of Lovat. He was said to have presided over the slaughter of a huge herd of cattle at *'Bun an Sgamhaidh'* or 'place of refuse'. Folk tradition says that the two large mounds of stones near *Upper Feorlig* are the burying places of the armies of MacLeods and MacDonalds who, in one of their many battles, fought to the last man. As no young men were left to dig the graves, all that could be done by the women was to cover the two sets of dead with two piles of stones. Archaeologists tell us that this cannot be true, as these are chambered cairns from Neolithic times. There are at least five such chambered cairns around *Loch Bracadale*.

Feorlig, as we mentioned in chapter two, means 'farthing land', possibly because it was so fertile that the plots, although sub-divided, were capable of sustaining a family. It is likely that this is where 'MacLeod's Farm', visited by Johnson and Boswell, was situated. They called here on 21st September 1773 on their way from the Castle to their next accommodation at *Ullinish House*.

The *Bracadale* district, in the 1700s, became well known for its exports of quality black cattle and even as late as 1840 an annual 450 head were driven south from this district alone and several thousands from the Western Isles and other parts of Skye were walked through the island to the *Kylerhea* crossing. During the Napoleonic Wars these cattle were particularly profitable.

The Industry was first begun by the noted warrior and bard *Domhnull MacIain 'ic Sheumais* and was initially opposed by the other tacksmen who thought him a fool to so demean himself! It is interesting that the Gaelic word, *cliaranach* (man of renown), denotes both a bard and a swordsman. Both these professions were held in high regard in Celtic society, but stocksmen and tillers of the soil were despised! When news of his first venture reached King James IV in Edinburgh, he is reputed to have said: *"I have in Scotland a thousand men daring enough to drive cattle from the south to the north (cattle stealing) but only one, it seems, with the courage to drive the northern cattle south again."* This Donald MacDonald of *Kingsburgh* was indeed brave, to purchase cattle here in MacLeod country and turn a good penny profit. He had married the daughter of MacLeod of *Gesto* who was reputed to have kept the finest cattle on the island – gifted to the family by the fairies!

By the mid 1800s the sheep and wool industry was beginning to make large profits for the tacksmen around the

Loch, but the human population had declined in *Bracadale* from 1,842 in 1841 to 929 in 1881. 4500 sheep were sold yearly. Prices at that time were £7 for a horse, £6 10s for a cow, £1 for a cheviot sheep and 16s 6d for a blackfaced ewe with lamb at foot. Because the price of wool was high, flocks of wedders (castrated male sheep) were kept on some hirsels. Wool growth is superior on male animals, as most of the nutrition absorbed by ewes goes to the developing lamb.

At *Caroy* are the remains of the Episcopalian St. John the Baptist's Chapel, built in 1837/38, and the little cemetery attached to it. This burial ground is of particular interest to me as my maternal great and great-great grandparents are buried here. Alexander Watt 1811-1894 and his wife Georgina Sutherland 1814-1884 lived at *Vatten House* as did their daughter Dolina Daisy Watt 1850-1936 who later married William Ford Porteous 1848-1911. Family tradition gives a particular reason for their burial here. Alexander, Georgina and all their family were born at Durness in Sutherlandshire. Alexander was a shepherd there and came to Skye as the Sheep Manager at *Balmeanach Farm* following the clearance of that township. They lived in the accommodation provided at *Balmeanach* until Alexander's retiral, but then moved in with their daughter Dolina, whose husband William, a 'retired mariner of independent means' had purchased *Vatten House*. It was 'expected' that incomers be buried in St. John's Churchyard rather than the parish cemetery at *Struan*!

The congregation of St Columba's Episcopal Church Portree paid for a boundary wall to be built around St John's in 1959. The balance of the cost was borne by Colonel Roger Swire and his wife, the author, Otta Swire in memory of their parents, Herbert and Evelyn Swire (a MacDonald of *Ord*) and William and Flora Tarn (a Robertson of *Greshornish*). Both Otta Swire and her husband are also buried here, surrounded by myriads of the snowdrops she loved, and so often wrote about.

Most poignant of all, is the gravestone to their granddaughter:

Flora MacDonald Margaret Swire
Born December 22nd 1964
Tragically killed on
Pan Am Flight 103
Over Lockerbie
December 21st 1988
Loved, remembered
and longed for always.

How very sad – on the eve of her 24th birthday! This gravestone connects "These Quiet Stones" with World events and reminds us of the supreme Christian example of forgiveness shown by Flora's father Dr. Jim Swire, spokesman for the UK bereaved parents.

Also at *Caroy* is the *Lag Buidhe* the mustering place for the armies of Clan MacLeod. They gathered here before their decimation at the Battle of Worcester in 1651 and again in 1745. On the latter occasion, only some 400 to 500 men appeared. Although both Norman MacLeod of MacLeod and Sir Alexander MacDonald had encouraged Bonnie Prince Charlie to come over to Scotland, they vacillated for fear of failure and confiscation of their estates, and those 500 men set out from Skye *'with white cockades in their bonnets'*, thinking that they were to join the Prince, only to discover that they were to fight against him. Donald MacLeod of Bernera, 'The Old Trojan' had realised this and had addressed his Chief with due deference. *"I place at your disposal the twenty men of your tribe who are under my immediate command and, in any other quarrel, I would not fail to be at their head, but in the present juncture I must go where a more imperious duty calls me."* He joined the Prince's army!

After the *Rout of Moy* many of the 'Hanoverian' MacLeods and MacDonalds 'melted into the hills' and quietly made their ways back home. Only about 150 MacLeods, under the command of the committed Loyalist, MacLeod of *Talisker*, continued on to Culloden.

Although past the prime of life 'The Old Trojan' set off on his own and joined Prince Charles on his retreat from Derby and narrowly escaped death at Culloden. For a time he hid from the Hanoverian troops in a cave at *Ulladale* in the forest of North Harris and latterly in a cave on *Toe Head* at *Northton*, South Harris. While in Harris he was attended by a young boy, John Martin. In the Inverness Courier of 25th March 1846 is a note, *"The death is recorded from Harris of a patriarch, John Martin, who was said to be 112 years old. As a boy he attended MacLeod of Berneray when in hiding after Culloden."*

Donald MacLeod was eventually restored to his estate in Berneray and the 'Old Trojan' became one of the wealthiest landholders in the west of Scotland. In his 75th year he married his third wife by whom he had nine children and died in his 90th year on 9th October 1781. In all, he had 29 children, several pre-deceasing him.

From *Caroy* the A863, 'MacLeod's Road', takes us on to *Ose*. It was here that *Màiri Mhòr* wrote her lovely song of love for the island of her youth, *'Nuair Bha Mi Og'*.

"Moch 's mi g-èirigh air bheagan èislein
Air madainn Chèitein 's mi ann an Òs
Bha sprèidh a geumnaich an ceann a chèile
'S a ghrian ag èirigh air Leac an Stòrr
Bha gath a boillsgeadh air slios nam beanntan
Cur tuar na h-oidhche na dheann fo sgòd
Is os mo chionn sheinn an uiseag ghreannmhor
Toirt na mo chuimhne nuair bha mi òg."

"Rising early with little sorrow
On a May morning when I was in Ose,
The cattle were lowing all together
As the sun was rising on Leac an Stoir;
A shaft of sunlight was beaming
Down on the mountain sides,
Quickly banishing the appearance of night,
And above my head sang the sprightly skylark,
Reminding me of when I was young."

While living and working in the Glasgow and Greenock area, Mairi would come back to Skye each summer to visit her good friend Margaret MacRae at Ose and on her final return to the island in 1882, she lived with Margaret *(Bean Ois)* until she moved to *Bothan Ceann na Coille*. In 1890 Margaret returned to Australia where she had spent her childhood. Mairi composed an 18 verse poem in her honour.

"Bidh mise ri smaointinn
Tric air Beann Òis,
'S nam bithinn ri taobh,
Cha bhithinn fo bhròn."

"I often think of Bean Os
And if I was beside her
I would not be sorrowful."

When Johnson and Boswell visited *Loch Bracadale* they were taken on an excursion to visit a large cave famous for *Mactalla,* the echo. On that particular day the echo was absent! As is still the case in Skye, the weather was blamed! Too much rain had fallen and the damp soil had dulled the echo. Boswell's caustic comment was, *"Such are the excuses by which the exaggerations of Highland narratives are palliated."* Because there are so many large caves hereabouts, it is now difficult to distinguish which one they visited. There is a large cave and sea-stack near *Harlosh Point* which is one of several in Skye called *Uamh an Oir* or Cave of Gold. Beyond *Idrigill Point* is *Uamh a'Choinnleir*, Candlestick Cave, but there are lots of other caves and natural arches on the islands of *Wiay, Tarner* and *Oronsay*. On the shores of *Loch Bracadale* Johnson saw his first mussels and limpets, *'in their natural state'*, and Boswell caught his first cuddy.

Our next ports of call are the *Eabosts* (*Eabost* and *Eabost West*), which are served by separate roads. Between the two is the former township of *Colbost* where was the home of my great grandfather Peter MacKinnon 1811-1885. Born in *Elgol*, Peter came to this area as shepherd for the farms of *Ullinish* and *Eabost,* and married Margaret Young 1821-1854. There are now lots of progeny of those two in both *Ullinish* and *Struan* but also in several other parts of Skye and indeed, throughout the world.

Johnson and Boswell visited Ullinish House, *"a very good farmhouse of two stories"*, as guest of Mr. MacLeod the local Sheriff. Boswell was impressed with the garden and the trees, and when he walked out for his morning stroll he witnessed the ship *'Margaret of Clyde'* sailing by with a number of emigrants on board.

Their excursions that day were to *Dùn Beag* and to the *Ullinish* souterrain. When Pennant visit the *Dùn Beag* in 1770 he recorded the height of the walls as 18ft high but now they are perhaps only 10ft to 12ft due to removal of quality building stone. Johnson speculated as to how the enormous flat stones which covered the entrance passage could have been so maneouvered. *"They seem heavier than could have been placed where they now lie, by the naked strength of as many men as might stand about them. They were probably raised by putting long pieces of wood under them, to which the action of a long line of lifters might be applied. Savages, in all countries, have patience proportionate to their unskilfulness, and are content to attain their end by very tedious methods."*

He concluded that these brochs were places for the former inhabitants in lawless times to keep their cattle safe at night from their marauding neighbours. Ann MacSween in her book *"Skye"*, says, *"Brochs would have been of limited use for a community whose animals were being pillaged, as it is unlikely that there would have been enough room inside to house sheep and cattle."* Certainly there would be a strict time limit on keeping cattle there due to the absence of wells and the large distances over which fodder and water would have to be carried.

Between 1914 and 1920, *Dun Beag* was excavated by Countess Hanna von Etinghausen, the daughter of an Austrian Baron. She had married Norman MacLeod the 25th Chief. He died in 1895 and she re-married Count Vincent Baillet de Latour. Both she and her new husband continued to spend summers in Skye living at the house known as 'The Beehive' at *Uiginish*. My mother remembered the couple working at *Dun Beag*. The objects which were recovered, suggested permanent occupation during Iron Age times, bone implements, glass beads, pottery and a steatite lamp as well as arrowheads and combs. *Dun Beag* is the best preserved of all Skye's twenty or so brochs, although less elaborate defensive duns are much more numerous.

The *Ullinish* souterrain can be seen to this day but the beehive dwellings or hut circle which once surrounded it have disappeared into the moss and other vegetation. These underground 'dwellings' are variously called 'erd-houses' or 'earth-houses' and probably belong to the Iron Age, although Johnson emphatically states, *"They are not the work of an age much ruder than the present; for they are formed with as much art as the construction of a common hut requires. I imagine them to have been places only of occasional use, in which the Islander, upon a sudden alarm, hid his utensils, or his clothes, and perhaps sometimes his wife and children."* Most authorities now agree that these were over-winter storage areas for grain and would only in emergency be used for human shelter.

To find this souterrain, these days, can be quite problematic. The sign, erected by the Museum Service, is indeed still in position, but the prevailing southwest wind has obliterated all the printing.

Close to this spot, but nearer the coast are two good examples of chambered cairns. Most experts agree that these tombs are from an earlier age than the brochs or souterrains and, for an unknown reason, ceased to be built after about 2000BC, so most chambered cairns belong to the late Neolithic period or early Bronze Age.

We now proceed to *Struan* (G. Little Stream) with its local school, grocery shop, outdoor clothing factory/shop, restaurant, two churches and garage. My maternal grandfather, Duncan and his brother Neil, both master joiners, built two semi-detached houses, *Creagard* and *Craiglea* for their respective families at *Struan*. Here my mother was born in

1909, one of a family of eight. At the little school, the children, all native Gaelic speakers, were punished if they spoke a word of their own language either in the classroom or the playground. Not so now, when many of Skye's Primary schools have Gaelic Medium Units where the language of instruction is their native one.

By the side of *Alltan Duilich* which runs down from the township of *Totarder* to the sea at *Balgown* is the ancient burial ground of *Struan*. Most historians maintain that this was the site of the ancient church of St. Assynt, the patron saint of this part of Skye, but Lucy Sanderson Taylor, in her research into churches in the area, claims that there was no such saint and that *"a reference in 1632 to the chapel of Assind in Brakadail is the Norse áss endi, meaning ridge end"* and that the ancient church was above the valley on the ridge of moor between Portree and Struan. She further states that *Assynt* in Sutherlandshire has a similar derivation.

Be that as it may, there is a very old burial ground by the *Alltan Duilich*. Here are buried some of Skye's most famous clergymen of the nineteenth century, Rev. John Shaw, Rev. James Ross and, of course, Rev. Roderick MacLeod, *Maighstir Ruaraidh*.

Rev. Roderick, while still an ordained missionary at *Lynedale*, visited Rev. John Shaw in the *Bracadale Manse*. Here he saw a copy of Bellamy's 'Christian Religion Delineated' and Chalmers' 'Lectures on Romans' on Shaw's bookshelf. Having read these he became concerned about his own spiritual condition. The resulting change in his life and preaching soon became apparent to many of his clerical associates who *"often spoke with bitterness about evangelical religion"*. Shortly after Rev. Shaw died, *Maighstir Ruaraidh* was presented to the *Bracadale* parish by MacLeod of MacLeod. He later claimed that his appointment here was on account of his ability *"as a good shot"*, which appealed to the landowning aristocracy, rather than his godliness or preaching ability.

We also find here simple memorials made, appropriately, from small pieces of gabbro, to two of the pioneers of *Cuillin* mountaineering, Dr. Norman Collie and Skye's own John MacKenzie.

Norman Collie was Professor of Organic Chemistry at Manchester University and first came to Skye in 1886 to fish on the *Sligachan River*. He fell in love with the island and his interest in walking the hills soon developed into attempts at some of the most difficult climbing routes in the *Cuillin*. Although his new-found climbing skills took him to the Alps and Himalayas, Collie always regarded the rough gabbro of the *Black Cuillin* as his favourite climbing rock. *Sgurr Thormaid* and *Collie's Ridge* are named after him. Following retirement, Collie spent his remaining years at *Sligachan Hotel*. When he died there in November 1942, his last wish, to be buried beside his good friend and mountain guide John MacKenzie, was granted.

John MacKenzie was born at *Sconser* in 1856 and became the first local mountain guide. Collie said of him that he was *"the only real climbing guide in the Swiss mould"* that Britain had produced. He climbed *Sgurr nan Gillean* at the age of ten and from then he was hooked. For the next fifty years he led expeditions from *Sligachan*. He was with the Pilkington brothers when they made the first ascent of the *Inaccessible Pinnacle* and was the first man to set foot on *A' Cioch* in Corrie Lagan; indeed his gravestone is shaped to represent the *Cioch* on *Sgurr Sgumain* but it is *Sgurr Mhic Coinnich* that is named after him.

Many of those guided by him have sung his praises. Sheriff Valentine said; *"He always retained his independence. He had his croft and could live without the tourists. His stride was long and his eye keen. When his companions, wearied by a hard day, had sat themselves down with relief, they would see him set forth in the dusk for the three-mile trudge to his cottage, as fresh as a youth in his prime and that when he was already far on in his sixties. He had the characteristic of the Highlander; the courtesy joined to self-respect that is the heritage of the clans. His accent to the end smacked something of the Gaelic speaker and the turns of his phrases showed in what language his thoughts had been moulded. Always alert, always cheerful, he was an excellent companion, but it was when the mist came down on the wet rocks that his worth was known. Scottish cragsmen may be content and proud to have him as a leader and a memory."*

Collie said of him; *"As a companion on a long summer day he was perfect. Always cheerful, keenly alive to everything – the wild birds, the deer on the hillside, the fish in the rivers and all natural things. There is no one who can take his place. Those who knew him will remember him as a perfect gentleman who never offended by word or deed. He has left a gap that cannot be filled. There was only one John, simple-minded, most lovable, and without guile. May he rest quietly in the little graveyard at Struan!"*

John died at the age of 76 in 1933. D. F. Rankine said of him:

"Sing the praise of doughty John,
Lord of crag and boulder,
Peak and gully, slab and scree,
Pinnacle and shoulder;
Sure of foot and keen of eye,
Cheery words to hail us;
Ready still with rope and hand
When the footholds fail us."

This old churchyard of *Struan* is where my own grandparents, Duncan MacKinnon 1854 - 1931 and Georgina Porteous 1880 – 1958, and, we think, my great grandparents, Peter MacKinnon and Margaret Young (already mentioned) are buried.

The delightful *Loch Beag* has a fishing pier by the remains of the *Old Inn*. In recent years the anchorage has again become popular with the yachting fraternity who are rediscovering many of the lovely spots within *Loch Bracadale*. Fishing for lobsters, crabs and langoustines continues, and these, along with hand-picked dived scallops are now readily available in the quality restaurants in this area.

It was here that an enterprising local man, Ally Willie Nicolson, published Skye's first ever newspaper in 1951. The *'Clarion of Skye'* started as a single stencilled sheet priced at $2^1/_2$d but grew to sixteen pages. It continued until 1957 when the editor's illness led to its demise. The 74 issues, kept bound at *'Dualchas'*, the Skye Museum Service, make for very interesting reading.

From *Struan* our route takes us around by *Loch Beag*, either by the modern causeway beneath *Dun Diarmid* or via the township of *Amar* (the trough or river of the rocky channel). The old road goes uphill to *Coillore* (the wood of gold), but the double track main road goes around *Boust Hill* to *Gesto Farm*. The Council have thoughtfully provided lay-bys here for visitors and locals alike, as the views from here are truly spectacular; west across *Loch Bracadale* to *Idrigill Point* and *Rubha nan Clach*, and south across *Loch Harport* to the magnificent *Black Cuillin*.

The former *Gesto House* in the sheltered bay, the home of the MacLeods of *Gesto*, has long gone. It was one of Skye's earliest slated houses, described as having been *'thatched with slate, held on with heather nails'*. Otta Swire remembers it *'covered with flowering creepers, roses and honeysuckle'*. As always, she remembers to recall the carpets of snowdrops, *'brought from the Crimea'*. In Chapter 4, we mentioned a dispute between the *Gesto* MacLeods and their Chiefs, which eventually led to Court Action won by Neil MacLeod of *Gesto* against the 24th Chief. In 1825 the Chief exacted revenge and refused to renew his lease so that the family lost what had been their traditional homeland for 500 years. Indeed they had not needed to pay rent on this estate until 1674 as this small portion of Skye had belonged outright to the *Gesto* cadet of the Clan.

The former township of *Sumardale* was granted as a tack to *Niall Og* (Young Neil Beaton) son of *Fearchar Lighiche*

(Farquhar the surgeon) in recognition of their skills as doctors and herbalists to MacLeod of MacLeod. In turn, Neil guaranteed that in each future generation, at least one from the family would study medicine. It is interesting that, nowadays, *Gesto* and *Sumardale* are farmed by descendants of the Beatons, and family members do indeed follow the medical profession.

John Beaton (or Bethune) the eldest son of Angus and grandson of Neil became a *"learned divine and an able physician"*. He became the Protestant minister of *Bracadale* in 1689 and was *"first to dispense communion in the Presbyterian form"*.

Gesto again features in a despicable event of Highland history which cast suspicion on the reputation of Norman 22nd Chief of MacLeod and Sir Alexander 15th Chief of MacDonald. Concern had been expressed for some years, between the Jacobite Rebellions of 1715 and 1745 that young people from the west coast of the mainland and from the islands were going missing. In the past, disappearances of this kind were attributed to Spanish Pirates, but they had ceased to operate around the British coast. A tale was told of a young girl from *Gesto* who went to the shore to gather the lichen *crotal,* with which to make dye for cloth. When she failed to return, it was assumed that she had been abducted and spirited away. Some years later, a Skyeman called by chance at a certain Canadian farmhouse. The young lady who came to the door did not understand him when, in English, he asked her the time. Having tried in French and German without success, he resorted to his native Gaelic. The lady leapt for joy and replied *"Tha e àm cròdhadh chaorach mu dhà thaobh Beinn Duagraich."* (*"It's the time for gathering the sheep from both sides of Ben Duagraich."*) She then proceeded to quote a rhyming list of place-names from the *Gesto* area. She explained that she had been smuggled aboard a ship, had been joined by several other prisoners from Lewis and Harris, and had been brought to Canada. She was the *Gesto* crotal-gatherer! Dr. Sorley MacLean in his epic poem *'The Cuillin'* uses this tale as an example of the hardships suffered by the emigrants, the poor and other 'less fortunate of this world'.

*"Fhuair mise diachainn gun fhaochadh
on latha chuireadh mi air Long nan Daoine.
Bha mi 'n Geusto a'buain maoraich
an uair a ghlacadh mi 's mi 'm aonar.*

....

*'S ioma nì thig air na bochdan
ach cha d' fhuiling neach mo lochd-sa,
ged bha mi sona nuair bha mi òg,
a dh'aindeoin bochdainn, an Dùis MhicLeòid.*

....

*Saothair, acras, fannachd, tàmailt,
b' iadsan a' chuibhrionn a bha 'n dàn dhomh;
agus a chaoidh cha ruig mi fàire
om faic mi Loch Harport 's taigh mo mhàthar
far an robh cridhealas is gàire
aig luaidhean ri linn mo chàirdean;
agus chan fhaic mi an Cuilithionn cràcach
ag éirigh thar Minginis mo shàth-ghaoil."*

"I knew hardship without respite from the day I was put on the Ship of the People.
I was in Gesto gathering shellfish when I was seized, being alone.

....

Many a thing comes on the poor but no one has suffered my hurt, though I was happy when I was young, in spite of poverty, in the Land of MacLeod.

....

Toil, hunger, faintness, shame, those were the portion in fate for me; and never may I reach a horizon to see Loch Harport and my mother's house where there was warmth and laughter at waulkings in the time of my people; and I may not see the horned Cuillin rising above Minginish of my full love."

Not long after, in 1739, 'The William', a ship laden with 96 people bound for America, put in to the port of Donaghadee in Co. Down. The Captain, William Davidson, disembarked his 'passengers' and put them under armed guard in a barn while the ship was checked by the authorities for its fitness to undertake an Atlantic crossing. Some of the prisoners escaped and the plot was exposed. Norman MacLeod of *Unish,* son of Donald MacLeod, 'The Old Trojan', had made the arrangement with Davidson to capture fit young people from the islands and to sell them as slaves in the Americas. Both MacLeod and

Davidson escaped justice, many believing that they could have revealed that the Clan Chiefs were behind the enterprise and that this was not the first occasion on which the 'arrangement' had been made. The incident has been called *'Soitheach nan Daoine'* ('The Ship of the People'). Sir Alexander's wife, Lady Margaret, wrote a letter to the Lord Justice Clerk, on her husband's behalf, in an attempt to silence the rumours.

"In harvest last we were pretty much alarmed with accounts from different corners of this and the neighbouring isles, of persons being seized and carried off aboard a ship which put in to different places on this coast. Sir Alexander is both angry and concerned that some of his own people were taken in this manner, but could not learn who were the actors in this wicked scrape till the ship was gone."

As the rumours continued, Sir Alexander himself confided in his lawyer MacKenzie of Dulvine, *"Last year MacLeod and I, in conversation we had, were regretting that we could not light on some effectual method for preventing theft on this isle ... and we agreed at last that the best method was to get some fellow that would take them on board a ship and carry them over to the Plantations ..."*

None of those on *'The William'* were criminals! Sixty were women and children, thirty six were men, none of whom had been convicted of any crime!

Norman of *Unish* did not show face in Skye for some years but remained in Ireland. At the '45, still in favour with his own Chief, he was commissioned with the rank of Captain when the MacLeods were mobilised in support of the Government. We are told that after Culloden *'none was so zealous in pursuit of his father, who was a rebel'*!

CHAPTER 9

Minginish
Of Wool and Tweed

We must now drive south on 'MacLeod's Road' via *Sumardale*, *Meadale* and *Drynoch* to the head of beautiful *Loch Harport*. We understand that it was the famous Thomas Telford who gave advice for this road section from *Dunvegan* to *Sligachan* in 1805, but it was not completed until 1829 at a cost considerably higher than the estimate. MacLeod of MacLeod paid £15,000 of the final £40,000. The engineer was Joseph Mitchell and the finished article was described as *"the most perfectly constructed under the Commissioners for Highland Roads and Bridges"*. The bridge at *Allt Coir' a' Ghobainn* had, at that time, the highest arch in Scotland. It was replaced by a simple culvert when the road was upgraded and renamed A863, in the late 1960s.

When Duncan MacPherson, who wrote *'Gateway to Skye'*, passed this way just after World War II, he noted that the road had only been tarred along its centre, thus reducing the useful width, and that grass had encroached on either side. He speculates that Inverness County Council had been conned by the Government, suggesting that they had accepted a 90% grant for half the road, believing this to be better than a 50% grant for the whole width!

Drynoch is variously interpreted as 'the place of thorns' or 'the Druids' place'. Usually, when there is a connection with the Druids, there are bee-hive dwellings in evidence, as in *Lonfearn* in *Trotternish,* but, as these seem to be absent, and the steep slope on the east of the loch is festooned with brilliantly yellow flowering gorse for most months of the year, and named *Bràigh Coille na Droighniche,* the former name seems more likely.

Here at *Drynoch* is the Cemetery of *Trien.* This name is very likely derived from the Trinity, to whom a former church was dedicated, but some believe it to come from the Gaelic word for the corncrake, *traon.* These birds could still be heard here in the 1970s, but an earlier hay-mowing season has resulted in fewer corncrakes nesting in Skye's fields.

Leaving the main A863 road we turn right to cross the *River Drynoch* and come into MacAskill territory. *"Originally the MacAskills were a family of Norse origin (Askill) who came to Britain with an invasion fleet about 1,000 years ago. They settled first in Ireland but, following a feud that developed there, they removed themselves to Skye. In those times the Hebrides belonged to the kingdom of Man and the Isles, owing ultimate allegiance to the kings of Norway. According to tradition the king of Man appointed the MacAskills keepers of Dunscaith Castle in Sleat. When Norse rule ended in 1266 the MacAskills threw in their lot with the MacLeod Clan".* So says the website 'MacAskilling.com' which gives detailed genealogy of this most interesting Skye family. Frances Tolmie, who did research on her ancestors, claimed that the early MacAskills were noted warriors and that they *"treasured a sword which had been used by the MacAskill of the day at the Battle of Bannockburn in 1314".* Indeed the military tradition continued through the generations. Kenneth MacAskill, in 1795, was an officer in the Royal Fencible Highland Regiment and served for five years with them in Ireland. His son became General Sir John MacAskill (1780 – 1845).

The first MacAskill in MacLeod's service, *Dòmhnall Dubh,* or Black Donald, was given the title Lieutenant of the Coast and was in charge of a team of watchmen who kept a lookout for the approach of sea-borne enemies. It was from this Black Donald that the MacAskills received their name *Clann Dhomhnaill Duibh* (Clan of Black Donald). Tradition says that the well-known pipe tune *'Piobaireachd Dhomhnaill Duibh'* (Black

Donald's March) was composed by a MacCrimmon in honour of his master's watchman. He had two sons, Donald and Allan. Allan was granted the lands of *Talisker*, but a later MacLeod chief removed his descendants to *Glendale* to make way for a cadet of the MacLeod clan who had coveted their tack. The *Glendale* branch failed to prosper there and seem to have disappeared as a distinct family long ago. Not so the descendants of Donald. He was given lands around *Glenbrittle* and based himself at *Rubh' an Dùnain*, the better to continue his family's coast-watching duty. They continued here until 1864.

By 1700 seven of the large farms of *Minginish* were held on tack from the MacLeods by MacAskills, descendants of Donald. In 1770 the ten sons of Finlay MacAskill of *Buaile an Tùir* were among the first 'voluntary' Skye emigrants to America. The farm of *Buaile an Tùir* (tower paddock) is on the west side of *Glenbrittle*. It is likely that it was the site of a lookout tower used for signalling purposes by the Macaskills, as it is in line of sight with the fort at *Rubh' an Dùnain*. There were similar watchtowers at the mouth of *Loch Eynort* and on the coast near *Talisker*. Much of the MacAskill history is recorded by Dixie and Malcolm MacAskill in their book, '*MacAskills in North America 1770-1984*'.

By 1824 the Skye MacAskills occupied most of *Minginish* and their farms had prospered, mainly due to the breeding of black cattle. Others of the family had taken over tacks in the Island of Berneray (see Giant MacAskill Chapter 6).

Sheep farming came to Skye at the start of the 19th century and it has been claimed that it was first introduced by the MacAskills. The new breeds were branded with an 'S' and known in the district as '*Rhundunan*' sheep. As early as 1803 a Kenneth MacAskill was complaining to fellow farmers about the cost and delays in getting customs clearance for shipment of wool to Liverpool. A few years later an agricultural survey reported, "*Sheep have lately been introduced as farm stock at Rhundunan, Gesto and Tallisker and they promise to do well. They are indeed the only proper stock for the Cuillin mountain districts.*"

From *Drynoch* we drive by *Satran* and *Merkadale* to the famous *Talisker Distillery* at *Carbost*.

The distillery was opened in 1830 by the brothers Hugh and Kenneth MacAskill who were granted a 60-year lease by MacLeod of MacLeod although, as we quoted earlier, it was not given a welcome by *Maighstir Ruaraidh* who said it was *"one of the greatest curses that, in the ordinary course of Providence, could befall this or any other place".*

The MacAskills eventually sold out to Roderick Kemp and Co. In 1895 *Dailuaine-Talisker Distilleries Limited* was formed and in 1900 they built a pier and railway to carry materials to and from the distillery. Barley for the brew, coal for the boilers and empty, used, sherry casks were carried here by puffer and the full barrels were taken away. The all important water comes from springs on the hillside but cooling water for the stills is taken from the local stream. In 1914, the company received a feu-charter to confirm that they were permitted to cut local peat, whose fragrant smoke flavours the malting grain. In 1916 The Distillers Company took over, but it is now owned by the giant Diagio Company. After a severe fire in 1961, the distillery was quickly re-built and, apart from that short break, it has produced whisky continuously from 1830 to the present day. Most of the spirit goes to the Scotch Whisky blending houses, but a significant proportion is bottled as *Talisker Pure Highland Malt* and has won several prizes as one of the world's top Single Malt Whiskies.

Over the years the distillery has had some notable visitors including many members of the Royal Family. A Mr. A. Barnard who visited in 1887 described how he saw the local women cutting and bringing in the peat. He was also impressed with the situation of the distillery:

"The Talisker Distillery stands at the foot of a beautiful hill, in the centre of the smiling village of Carbost, which, after the bare and rugged track we had passed through was an agreeable change, and seems quite a lively place. On the broad slopes of the hills, which were covered with crofters' holdings, husbandmen were busy tilling the soil; while at the Distillery below and the

village which surrounds it, all was life and motion. Driving along we were struck with the picturesque situation of the Distillery, which stands on the very shore of Loch Harport, one of the most beautiful sea-lochs on this side of the island."

Following his visit here in 1880, Robert Louis Stevenson mentioned Talisker in 'The Scotsman's Return from Abroad'.

"The king o' drinks, as I conceive it,
Talisker, Isla, or Glenlivet."

Andrew Dempster in his book *'Skye 360'* quotes a description of the taste of *Talisker* which he had heard: *"intense, peppery, pungent, peaty, powerful, seaweedy, sweet-and-sour and building to a warm finish after initially exploding in the mouth."*

Keith McGinn, Skipper of the puffer *'Polarlight'*, which was one of the last puffers to discharge coal at *Carbost Pier* says in his book 'Last of the Puffermen': *"If you are ever in Carbost and tied up at the pier, on the cliff face there is an underground spring running through the cliff into a small man-made pool. The water is the sweetest and coldest I have ever tasted, even on the hottest days. It is always ice-cold and in a glass of Talisker seems to add to the flavour. Lovely!"* In spite of this advice, many would regard it as sacrilege to add water to a Single Highland Malt!

McGinn tells of delivering 330 tonnes of coal from Ayr to *Carbost* in 1982. The steel hatches were opened on their arrival at 6.00am and they began discharging the coal at 7.00 and had completed the operation and battened down the hatches by 7.00pm. On his first visit to *Carbost* on the much smaller *'Lady Isle'* in 1967, the full cargo of 130 tonnes had taken one-and-a-half days of 14 hours, with shovels, to complete! Things had changed greatly in 15 years!

Things have indeed changed; in summer time *Loch Harport* is now alive, not with puffers, steamers and coasters but with visiting yachts anchored beneath that glorious view of the *Black Cuillin*, and the *Talisker Awards*, sponsored by *Diagio*, have encouraged local businesses in their efforts to make Skye **the** destination for that memorable holiday experience.

Carbostbeag and *Fernilea* are the next townships on our route. It was at *Fernilea House* that Johnson and Boswell landed, following their boat trip from *Uillinish,* and prior to their visit to *Talisker House.* The owner of *Fernilea* was an Alexander MacLeod. Boswell recalls; *"We had good weather and a fine sail this day. The shore was varied with hills, and rocks, and corn-fields and bushes, which are here dignified with the name of natural wood. MacLeod, expecting our arrival, was waiting on the shore, with a horse for Dr. Johnson. The rest of us walked!"* It was probably for this reason that Johnson described their host as; *"a worthy and sensible man".*

Portnalong (The Boat Harbour) has given its name to the wider district, and it was to this area that some seventy families from Scalpay, Lewis and Harris were moved in 1921 when the estate was purchased by the Board of Agriculture from MacLeod of MacLeod. These people were regarded by government planners as 'over-spill' from these highly populated islands. It is interesting that a few Skye families were moved to the mainland before the influx. This has led some writers to imply that the Agriculture Board were practising experiments in eugenics! The incomers built narrow houses with stone gables and walls and roofs of corrugated iron which were equipped with a proper bathroom! Each croft also had the essential loom-shed. The new school, also of corrugated iron, had a 'temporary look' but lasted well into the 1980s. Soon these families with *"that vivid Outer Hebridean capacity for enjoying social intercourse"* had established a community and a hand-loom industry. They sold the product as *Portnaskye Tweed* through Ballantyne Ltd of Peebles, who initially provided fifteen looms. Most of the output went to Japan and the USA. Production continued until 1968. Traditional plant dyes were used in the process. Alder bark (to give black), iris (to give ochre), bog myrtle (bright yellow), bracken (dark turquoise), sorrel (pale blue), crotal (russet red), goat's beard (pale brown). A dark chestnut was made from the common white water-lily and pine green from heather. One visitor in 1930 recorded seeing *"the most beautiful hues of wool I have ever set eyes upon".*

The Duke and Duchess of York visited *Minginish* in 1933, following the Elgin Hostel opening, and received the gift of a length of '*special Portnalong Tweed and a bottle of Talisker*'.

Fiscavaig (Fish Bay) was also one of the townships settled by the Outer Islanders and indeed, one of the original settlers, a young teenager at the time, having now attained her centenary, still lives here (2008) and enjoys singing the Gaelic songs and hymns of her childhood.

There is an interesting walk to a galleried dun from the *Ardtreck* road-end, and it can be continued out to the small lighthouse at Ardtreck Point where there are indications of a long departed community.

Between *Fiscavaig* and *Talisker* is the headland of *Rubha nan Clach*. Some say that it was here that a cow fell from the cliff and landed on a boat which was anchored beneath, others claim that the incident occurred near *Dunvegan Head*. Either way, the cow's owner and the owner of the boat were tenants of MacLeod of MacLeod. The particular chief of the time was *Alistair Crotach*. Both men complained to their chief, as the cow had been killed and the boat destroyed. Compensation was demanded and it was the duty of the Clan Chief to judge who should pay. At that particular time there was a short period of peace between *Alistair Crotach* MacLeod and *Donald Gorm* the Chief of the MacDonalds at *Duntulm,* and *Alistair Crotach* knew that the MacDonald chief often relied on the skilful judgements of *Taog Mor MacQueen*. This famous sage was sent for and he patiently listened to the arguments. The cow's owner stated that, if the boat had not been anchored beneath the cliff, his animal would have survived the fall into deep water and would easily have been able to swim to the gently sloping beach. The boat's owner maintained that his vessel was anchored in its usual position and would have remained undamaged if the cow had not landed on it. *Taog's* Solomon-like judgment was to the effect that *Alistair Crotach* should compensate both owners, as he was the proprietor of the cliff which was the common factor, and therefore the primary cause of the accident. The Chief paid up with good humour as this neatly solved his predicament.

From *Fiscavaig* there is a two-mile footpath through the *Huisgill Glen* to *Talisker*. I remember walking this way on one of the Field Club excursions from school. Memory tells me that most of these trips were blessed with excellent weather, but not this particular one. It was wet and blustery! A great shame because *Talisker* can be such a glorious place when the sun shines. The beach is composed of two coloured sands, black and white which can often form intricate patterns as the sea swirls them together. Seton Gordon wrote: *"In all the Isle of Skye there are few places more remote than Talisker. The old house stands beside the Atlantic, and north and south great precipices rise where yeasty torrents fall mightily from their birth-place among the mists to the thundering seas a thousand feet below."*

Samuel Johnson tells us that at *Talisker* ('the House of the Rock') he *"looked at no less than fifteen different waterfalls near the house in the space of about a quarter of an hour."*

Sorley MacLean's beautiful poem *Tràighean* (Shores), begins:

"Nan robh sinn an Talasgar air tràigh
far a bheil am bial mór bàn
a' fosgladh eadar dà ghiall chruaidh,
Rubha nan Clach 's am Bioda Ruadh,
Sheasainn-sa ri taobh na mara
ag ùrachadh gaoil 'nam anam
fhad 's a bhiodh an cuan a' lìonadh
camus Thalasgair gu sìorruidh:
Sheasainn an siod air lom na
tràghad gu 'n cromadh Priseal a
cheann àigich."

"If we were in Talisker on the shore
where the great white mouth
opens between two hard jaws,
Rubha nan Clach and the Bioda
Ruadh,

I would stand beside the sea
renewing love in my spirit
while the ocean was filling
Talisker bay forever:
I would stand there on the bareness
of the shore
until Prishal bowed his stallion head."

The more usual approach to *Talisker* is by road from *Carbost* through *Gleann Oraid*, as it is named on the map. The name was originally *Gleann fo Rathad*, the Glen Below the Road, and as you drive this way no further explanation is necessary!

Many visitors have come here over the years. Pennant, in 1790 says; *"Talyskir belongs to the chief of MacLeod, and in old times was always the portion of a second son; he enjoyed it in life, with a view of giving him the means of educating his children, who after that were left to the care of fortune."* He was rowed out in the bay to circumnavigate *"a pyramidal and reclining rock"*, *Stac an Fhucadair* (the Stack of the Fuller of Cloth) to the rhythm of a *iorram* (rowing song).

Dr Johnson writes; *"We passed two days at Talisker very happily, both by the pleasantness of the place, and the elegance of our reception."* His further comments are perhaps not so uplifting! *"Talisker is the place beyond all that I have seen from which the gay and the jovial seem utterly excluded, and where the hermit might expect to grow old in meditation, without possibility of disturbance or interruption."* The Doctor had, of course, sat out in the garden in the shade of a plane tree while Boswell had climbed *Preshal Mòr* *"a very high and rocky hill, whence there is a view of Barra, the Long Island, Bernera, the Loch of Dunvegan, part of Rhum, part of Raasay, and a vast deal of the Isle of Skye."* He did not climb *Preshal Beag*, which, in the nature of these things, is in fact more lofty than *Preshal Mòr*. Of course the same is true of *MacLeod's Tables*, *Healabhal Bheag* is the taller! Often the Gaelic reference to mountain size refers to bulk rather than height. Seton Gordon tells us that, following a storm in January 1927, seaweed was to be seen on the 1000 ft top of *Preshal Beag*!

John Knox, the fishery surveyor sailed to *Talisker* from *Ullinish*. He says; *"Before we could land at the Bay of Talisker, Mr MacLeod, though extremely corpulent, had, with his usual politeness reached the beach, from whence we were conducted, through a small, rich valley, to the seat of plenty, hospitality, and good nature."*

Louis Albert Necker De Saussure, Professor of Mineralogy and Geology at the University of Geneva, who grew to love Skye, and is buried in the Old Cemetery in Portree, was another of *Talisker's* visitors. On September 26th 1820 he wrote: *"Mr MacLeod of Talisker, being informed of our arrival in the Isle of Skye, sent horses and a guide to conduct us to his house, and after two hours route on wretched roads, we arrived at Talisker House, where we were received as ancient friends. This fine house, surrounded with trees, is situated at the bottom of a little valley, which opens on the south upon the sea; the environs are fertile, and well cultivated; a small rivulet, which takes its rise in the rocky and basaltic hills in the neighbourhood, runs, winding around the house, after forming a beautiful cascade, at the foot of which the road passes. During dinner, the piper played in the hall, and these romantic airs, for a long time resounded in the vaults of the castle of Talisker."*

The tales of Ossian recall that Cuthullin, son of Semo, and grandson of Cathbaid, was one-time Chief of Skye and had his castle at *Dunscaich*. He had come here from his native Ireland to learn, for seven years, the art of warfare from *Queen Sgathach*. This Cuthullin was another of *Talisker's* visitors – he **must** have been, as Cuchulainn's Well is here, near the track between the house and the shore! A tale is told that one of the *Talisker* MacLeods would only drink water if it was drawn from this well. On one particularly dark and stormy night his butler was instructed to bring some well water. Given the inclement conditions, the servant filled his bucket from the stream! On tasting the water, MacLeod was suspicious, but the butler stuck to his story that it was indeed pure well water. Old Talisker demanded that they both go to the well together. This done, the container was duly filled with the 'nectar' and both turned for home. The butler, realising that his negligence was about to be exposed, courteously allowed his master to precede him over the bridge and quickly exchanged the well water for some from the stream, as they passed. MacLeod concluded that *Cuchulainn's Well* had been bewitched.

Seton Gordon loved the wildlife of this coast and writes of a visit here in the month of April when purple sand-pipers were feeding on the rocks at low tide. They were so tame that it was possible for him to approach within a few feet of them.

"Where the sea-cliffs lean toward the strengthening sun there is already a profusion of spring flowers, and the scent of fields of primroses mingles with the tang of the seaweed. In little pockets on the bare rock the buds of the sea thrift are a deep glorious crimson. In damp niches the golden flower-heads of the rose root have already appeared, and the crimson lychnis mingles with the yellow carpet of primroses."

On his climb to *Biod Ruadh* he discovered, on the grassy ledge of the cliff, an ancient eyrie of a sea-eagle. By this time, 1929, all of Scotland's white-tailed sea-eagles had been killed off by landowners and sheep farmers. Seton Gordon did not live to see their restoration to these islands of the west. Those re-introduced to Mull in 1985 have been very successful and their progeny now hunt and nest in several of the Hebridean islands and west coast mainland but, although they are attracting bird-watching visitors in their thousands, some crofters are suffering losses of young lambs. Much larger and more powerful than the golden eagle, the sea-eagle can lift a lamb with ease, although their main diet consists of sea birds, mainly fulmar. The iconic view of these birds is of them skilfully catching fish, with their talons, from just beneath the surface of the sea, but sheep owners claim that they will also cleverly fly high with a lamb and drop it onto the rocks, before carrying it back, dead, to the eaglets on the eyrie. Rather than repeat the evil of destroying these creatures because of their failure to discriminate between what man regards as legitimate or illegitimate prey, arrangements are now underway to compensate stock-keepers for genuine losses.

Leaving *Talisker* we now drive to the crofting and foresting community on *Loch Eynort*. There is a very ancient settlement here at *Borline* with the remains of two churches. The older and smaller one was dedicated to St. Maelrubha, a monk who, like St. Moluag, also came from Ulster. Maelrubha's main church was on the mainland at Applecross, *A' Chomaraich* (the sanctuary), founded in 673, and it was here that he died in 722. The old *Borline* church is marked on maps as *Kilmoruy,* a corruption of the saint's name. The carving of an abbot on the high Celtic cross in the churchyard is said to be a portrait of Maelrubha, and a stone font, dated 1430, now in the Museum of Antiquities in Edinburgh, may also show a representation of the saint. Otta Swire tells us that this relic was 'rescued' by some fishermen from South Uist and given, for safe-keeping to their priest. After his death, the well-known antiquarist Alexander Carmichael arranged for it to be presented to the Society of Antiquaries.

In the churchyard are several ancient gravestones which confirm that this was a very important religious site for hundreds of years. It is said that the National Covenant of Scotland (*"to maintain the true religion and the King's majesty"*) was signed here by all the Clan Chiefs and principal men of Skye in 1642. It had originally been drawn up and *"subscribed by the King's Majesty and Household in 1580"* and re-instated by the General Assembly of 1639. It became an Act of Parliament in 1640 requiring signature by all those of *'rank and quality'*, but it took the commissioners a considerable time to get around the whole of Scotland. Of course they arrived at *Loch Eynort* by ship. The later, larger church ruin was probably in use at this time and its minister was Rev. John MacKinnon. The Synod of Argyll were so impressed by his indigence that they decided to confer on him *"twelve bolls of victual out of the vacant parishes of Kintyr"* in order to relieve his immediate wants.

The *Eynort Glen* has seen much forestry activity since World War II and there is currently a vast felling programme. The single-track, unmetalled road along the left side of *Loch Eynort* has been adopted by the Forestry Commission and leads to *Glen Brittle*. This is also the track to *Kraikinish*, made famous by Margaret MacPherson in her children's book "*The*

Rough Road". Margaret, born in Colinton, Edinburgh in 1908, was the daughter of Rev. Dr. Norman MacLean, the Queen's Chaplain in Scotland. A graduate of Edinburgh University, she surprised everyone by marrying a lowly crofter, Duncan MacPherson, whom she had met on holidays to her father's native Skye. In the 1930s, times were tough for Skye crofters, as they were for most people in this country, but Duncan and Margaret fought hard to make a success of their stock-rearing at remote *Kraikinish*. In time they had seven sons and Margaret wrote several children's books which were published in the 1960s when I was growing up. I loved these books because they had a distinctive Skye-flavour to which I could relate. My particular favourites were *'The Shinty Boys'* and *'The Battle of the Braes'*. Margaret was a member of The Taylor Commission which reported in 1954 into the state of crofting in the Highlands and Islands. When she disagreed with some of the commission findings, she had the courage to produce a minority report. One of Margaret's sons has continued to successfully farm the crofts and hills at *Eynort* and *Kraikinish*.

It may have been from *Eynort* that a famous kidnapping by Spanish Pirates took place, though some aver that it was from *Ullinish*. Throughout the 17th and early 18th Centuries there was a considerable fear of pirates, both foreign and native, around the coast of Skye and there were apparently several reports of abductions of young people. One spring morning, while gathering primroses by the loch side, a young girl named Gormul fell victim to this crime, and sad parents and friends were sure that she would never be seen again. Many years later a sailor, by the name of Alan MacAskill, a former playmate of young Gormul, returned home from many adventures at sea. He had a strange tale to tell, having been shipwrecked on an island in the West Indies. The surviving crew had been treated with kindness by the islanders. One day Alan and his companions were invited to the magnificent home of a Spanish nobleman and were regally entertained. In the course of the evening, Alan was astonished to hear a Gaelic song being sung by the wife of the Spaniard. It turned out that this was Gormul who had been Alan's neighbour when they were both children. Alan was able to tell her of her parents' welfare and promised to tell them of her new-found happiness in this idyllic home from which she had no intention of departing!

It seems very likely that this tale is apocryphal as it strikes a similar note to that of the *Bracadale* lass discovered in Canada praising *Beinn Duagraich*.

As our journey progresses we will likely have to backtrack to *Carbost* before taking the road to *Glenbrittle,* although, on one occasion I had permission from the Forestry Commission to drive a party of school pupils through the forestry tracks from one valley to the next. Locked gates prevent large-scale use of this convenience but the tracks make for ideal walking or cycling.

> "Grey winding glen with long grasses blowing,
> Swept by the storm wind and wet with the rain;
> Burns spraying high in the rush of their flowing,
> What would I give now to know you again!
>
> Hills of my heart, you have charms for beguiling
> All of God's world and his heavens above;
> Stern to the stranger, bleak and unsmiling,
> Bleak, but how dear to me – hills that I love."

Graham Dallas

Glenbrittle is another of Skye's lovely places and, like *Talisker,* it actually has a sandy beach! True, these are not the golden sands we associate with the Western Isles, but the *Glenbrittle* beach does have something in common with Barra's *Tràigh Mhòr*: it provided a landing place for aircraft. In pre-war days, not only ambulance planes would land here but there was a regular air-service from Glasgow! *Glenbrittle* is dominated by the Black Cuillin mountains and has been a climbing centre since the 19th Century. It still remains relatively unspoiled however, as the accommodation provided for the mountaineers consists of B&B, Youth Hostel, Climbers' Hut and campsite. Mercifully there are no hotels and, unlike The Lake District, it has not been commercialised. From 1932 until 1974 the MacRaes, at *Glenbrittle Lodge* boarding house, provided accommodation for climbers.

Many writers have had much to say about these mountains.

"The Cuillins in western Skye are among the great natural wonders of Europe, and although some of the peaks do require climbing skills there are other summits well within the capability of normal walkers, while wonderful views of the range can be had without expending any energy at all."

MacAskilling.com

"The Cuillin of Skye are unique in the British Isles and have long been popular with mountaineers. They are by far the most rugged mountains in the country and unlike any other range the tops are all connected by very narrow rocky ridges. It is seldom easy to get from one top to another and in some cases may be very difficult."

J.W.Simpson

"Below us lay the long curve of Glenbrittle, the road winding by the river, and, at the loch-side, a few crofts and a gleaming stretch of golden sands; beyond, heather slopes rose up to great gullies and black crags fading into mist. Again good fortune was with us. We at once secured accommodation at the post-office which receives mails twice a week and has no telephone. We looked out early next morning and shouted for joy when we saw the high Cuillin clear to their tops and the peaks piercing a sky still aglow in the blaze of a rising sun."

B. H. Humble

"There is no hill range in Scotland which varies so greatly in aspect as the Cuillin of Skye. With the weather their mood changes suddenly. They smile or are sad; they frown and are terrible. The dun wind from the Atlantic

reaches their blue, clear-cut spires, and immediately a mist curtain is drawn across them; before the coming of a storm they clothe themselves with a blue mantle of mystery. Then there are days when the Cuillin are alive with benign spiritual forces; when hill silence tells of many wonderful things; when hill, sun, and ocean glow with life and energy."

Seton Gordon

From these quotations it will be noticeable to all that the climbing and walking fraternity insist on speaking of the Cuillin rather than Cuillins. They also go 'for a walk on the hill' rather than 'in the hills'.

We will say more about these spectacular mountains in the next chapter, but meanwhile, a walk to *Rubh' an Dùnain* is called for. Of course there is no road, and the trek can be quite demanding and should not be attempted after heavy rain as the streams from the mountains become impassable. In good weather though, this is a spectacular day out. The total round trip is seven miles and five hours should be allowed to give a reasonably comfortable excursion.

Rubh' an Dùnain is the southernmost tip of the Minginish coastline. Terry Marsh says it is "a place for incurable romantics, a 'grianan' – sunny spot, or a secluded place for lovers. It is a place for wandering and exploration, a place of history where once a small community flourished." For clear directions of the paths to follow, you will not find better than Marsh's 'Walkers Guide' (see bibliography). Traces of cultivation become obvious as you approach the point, and Loch na h-Airde, the chambered cairn and the ruins of a substantial farmhouse come into view. This was the home of the MacAskills. Tradition says; "there was a MacAskill at Rubh' an Dùnain as long as there was a MacLeod at Dunvegan." The last was Hugh MacAskill who died in 1864. Beside the house, look out for the Saddle Stone (Clach na Diòllaid) which the MacAskill ladies used to mount their ponies. The fresh water loch often has herons at its edge and is a haven for ducks and swans. Only a few feet above sea level, you will spot the man-made channel where the birlinns were pulled up to a safe anchorage out of reach of the ocean. Near this channel is the fairly well preserved coast-watchers' signalling Dun from which the place gets its name. The chambered cairn to the north of Loch na h-Airde was extensively excavated in 1932 and turns out to have had a chequered history stretching back to use by the Beaker people some 3,000 years ago, and beyond. The settlement contained several buildings that would have served the community over the years. There is also evidence of a knapping industry. It is likely that the flint was collected from 'The Cave of the Arrows' beneath Sgurr an Fheadain (Chanter Peak) in Corrie na Creiche.

From *Rubh' an Dùnain* there are excellent views of the islands of Soay, Rum, Canna and Eigg.

> "And oh, for lone GlenBrittle
> And a view of the splinter'd ridge,
> And a climb on the rough hard gabbro,
> And a plunge from the lochan's edge;
> Then to stand by the crooning breakers
> And watch the setting sun,
> And see the shadows turning blue
> On Canna, Eigg, and Rhum."
> *Anon.*

CHAPTER 10
The Cuillin

The traverse of the main Cuillin Ridge involves about 10,000ft. of ascent and descent and makes for a very long and strenuous day even for the young and fit and it is not recommended unless individual sections have been previously reconnoitred. Weather in the high mountains can change rapidly and route-finding can be difficult in misty conditions. I recall Robin Murray showing us the antics of a compass needle, deflected by the iron content of the rocks, as we sat for picnic lunch beneath the *Inaccessible Pinnacle* on *Sgurr Dearg*. It caused me some concern as I had previously thought that the compass could always be relied upon. More modern technology can also be less than reliable. There are several mobile-phone black spots and even GPS, or its users, have experienced problems.

The most southerly mountain on the main Cuillin Ridge is *Gars Bheinn* and this is the usual starting point for the traverse, finishing at *Sgurr na Gillean*. (I had always understood the name of this summit as *'boys' peak'* and the boys referred to, as the pinnacles of Pinnacle Ridge, but the suggestion has been put to me that the *'Gill'* is the same as in the names *Idrigill* and *Lorgill*, meaning the ravine or edges between ravines. Local Gaelic pronunciation, using the thin 'L', suggests a different word than *'boys'* which uses a thick 'L'.)

Many of the mountains are named for their first conquerors or for other famous climbers who have enjoyed the Cuillin. *Sgurr Thearlaich* (Charles' Peak, 3208ft.), after Charles Pilkington of glass making fame, *Sgurr Alasdair* (to the side of the main ridge but the highest peak at 3257ft.), after Sheriff Alexander Nicolson, *Sgurr Mhic Coinnich* (MacKenzie's Peak 3111ft.) for John MacKenzie, the guide, *Sgurr Thormaid* (Norman's Peak 3040ft.), for Norman Collie. It is perhaps surprising that Laurence Pilkington, Charles' brother and William Wilson Naismith, who founded the Scottish Mountaineering Club, have been missed out, but there were lots of other pioneers in the late 1800s and they are all remembered in a list of first ascents.

Many of the individual climbs and routes have been given evocative names; *Goliath Buttress, Sanguinary Cracks, Foxes' Rake, Shining Cleft, Mantrap, Thunder Rib, Whispering Wall, Valkyrie, Styx, Varicose and Laceration.* One can imagine the weary but exuberant climbers dreaming up those names as they recount each move of hand and foot, while enjoying a pint in the *Sligachan Hotel.* It was due to *'a loose, overhanging chockstone in a chimney-like groove'* that Haworth and Ritchie on 17th May 1947 named their route **Hangover**, and not for any other reason!

Sorley MacLean's epic poem *An Cuilithionn* (The Cuillin) recalls many of the peaks on which Sorley himself walked and climbed, although it is essentially a political poem for a particular time, the prelude to war in 1939.

"Gun tigeadh dhomhsa thar gach àite bhith air do shlineannan àrda a' strì ri do sgòrnan creagach sàr-ghlas, mo ghleac ri d' uchd cruaidh sgorrach bàrcach."	"My place above every other place to be on your high shoulder-blades striving with your rocky great grey throat, wrestling with hard peaked surging chest."

As we walk back from *Rubh' an Dùnain* towards the *Glenbrittle* campsite we are able to identify the corries along this western side of the *Black Cuillin*. The first is *Coire nan Laogh* (calf corrie), followed by the two most important for the climbing fraternity *Coir' a' Ghrunnda* and *Coire Làgan*. These give access to *Sron Na Ciche* where the bulk of the severe and very severe climbs are to be found. As we travel, back on the road, up the valley the next corrie is *Coire na Banachdich*, opposite the *Glenbrittle Memorial Hut*. The curve of the great ridge means that *Coire a' Ghreadaidh* (corrie of torment) faces north-west and finally *Coire na Creiche* (corrie of the spoil) to the north. This last corrie is named for the great and final battle which took place between the Clans MacDonald and MacLeod. The final victory for the MacDonalds of Sleat brought to an end the two year 'war of the one-eyed woman' which was referred to in *'Like a Bird on the Wing'*.

Perhaps the most obvious feature in this corrie, that can be seen from the road, is *Waterpipe Gully* which cleaves the face of *Sgurr an Fheadain* (chanter peak) but there are other very interesting sights which require a little walking. The lovely short walk (20mins.) to the *Fairy Pools* on *Allt Coir a' Mhadaidh* is well worthwhile. These deep, turquoise-blue pools, separated by a series of waterfalls, are unusual and seem like magic. If you are willing to strike out onto the path which connects *Glenbrittle* to *Sligachan* (*Bealach a' Mhàim*) you may be able to identify some features which were of particular interest to Seton Gordon.

"The traveller may observe, near the Maam path, at the entrance to Coire na Creiche, what appears to be the moraine left by some glacier. Here a number of grassy mounds arise. The place is known to the old people as Tom nan Tighearnan (knoll of the lairds), and commemorates the historic Battle of Beinn a' Chuillin fought in 1601." He explains that *Donald Gorm Mòr MacDonald of Sleat*, crossed into MacLeod country, perhaps on a cattle raid. The MacLeod Chief, *Rory Mòr*, was in the south in conference with the Earl of Argyll, so it fell to the chief's brother *Alastair Og* of *Minginish* to gather the clan. *"The fight was waged all day with incredible obstinacy."* By nightfall many clansmen on each side lay dead but the MacDonalds could claim victory. *MacLeod of Minginish, "sheathed in armour"*, was wounded and taken prisoner with some thirty

other MacLeods but eventually released on the intervention of King James VI himself. It was at this battle that *Domhnall Mac Iain 'Ic Sheumais,* having slain many MacLeods, enhanced his reputation as a great swordsman, wielding his *'Lainnire Riabhach'* (the Evil Glittering One). Tradition speaks of him in the same tone as it does of the *Feinne* of antiquity: *"A neart mar dharg na coille, a chumadh cho direach ri giuthas na beinne,'s a chorp cho subailte ri cuilc nan lòn."* ("His strength like the oak of the forest, his form straight as the mountain pine, and his body lithe as the reed of the marshland.") He was also a bard (see Ch. 8) and composed the following lines on that occasion;

"Latha dhomh 's a' Chuilitheann chreagach;
Chuala mi phiob mhòr 'ga spreigeadh;
Nuallan a' chruidh laoigh 'ga freagairt;
Bha beul-sios air luchd an leadain,
Bha làrach am bròg 'san eabar;
'S iad Clann Dho-uill rinn an leagadh".

"One day I happed in rocky Cuillin;
I heard the great warpipe astrumming;
Lowing of milch kine responding,
Ill-luck befell the men of (long locks),
The imprints of their brogues in mire;
Clan Donald was responsible for their whelming."

One of the 'grassy mounds' on *Tom nan Tighearnan* is surmounted by a small commemorative cairn *Carn nan Tri Tormod* (Cairn of the Three Normans), where three MacLeod noblemen were interred. Four hundred years after the event, the cairn is now just a jumble of stones. A second cairn was pointed out to Seton Gordon as the burial place of the *MacAskill* of *Rubh' an Dùnain* and a hundred yards south of it he observed a number of flat stone slabs believed to be the graves of MacDonald victims of the fight. Gordon's knowledgeable informant was also able to show him another memorial a mile to the north where a wounded MacLeod, being carried homewards by a faithful servant, had succumbed to his wounds. Nowadays we expect our history to be in writing, whereas, even one hundred years ago, when Gordon trod this path, the older generation were very much the receptacles of knowledge from the past and the oral tradition was still powerful among some *sennachies* (story tellers).

According to tradition, within a year, the MacLeods and MacDonalds were reconciled, and *Rory Mòr* made a great feast at *Dunvegan* for *Donald Gorm Mòr*. The MacCrimmon of the day, the great Donald *Mòr* composed '*MacLeod's Welcome*' and Charles MacArthur replied with '*MacDonald's Salute*'.

Our return drive takes us back to the *Drynoch* road junction for our continued journey through *Glen Drynoch,* by *Crossal* to *Sligachan* (the place of the shells). This name is a Gaelic one, thought to be pre-Norse, but claims that there is a link with the Ossianic tales, seem to be based on rather thin evidence. The stories, 'translated' in MacPherson's poems, tell of the *Feinne* drinking wine out of scallop shells studded with gems; *"often did they feast in the hall, and sent round the joy of the shell"*, and describe Fingal himself as *"the King of generous shells"*. There is no doubt, however, that there are excellent scallops, as well as mussels, cockles, razor-fish and winkles still to be harvested in *Loch Sligachan*, and it was probably ever thus.

Sligachan was, of course, one of the main animal market centres for at least a hundred years. It is said that the first cattle market here was opened by the Chief, Colonel MacLeod of MacLeod on Wednesday 22nd October 1794. Derek Cooper's research tells us that; *"about 4,000 people attended the tryst and 1,400 head of cattle and 200 horses and ponies changed hands. All the Skye ponies sold were taken to work in the Lanarkshire coalfields. One of the most colourful sights at the fair was the huge tinker camp set up at nearby Crossal where music, song and dance continued all through the night."*

Sligachan Hotel was recognised as one of the most famous mountaineering centres in Europe in the late 19th Century when climbing was a sport of the 'nouveau riche', but now the popularity of the campsite is perhaps pre-eminent for accommodation, although the hotel provides meals and refreshments as well as a necessary wet-weather area. The hotel's Climbing and Fishing books have a wealth of history, recording peaks and salmon 'bagged'! Alexander Smith says: *"I baited at Sligachan – dined on trout which a couple of hours before were darting hither and thither in the stream."*

A recent collection of information from the *Sligachan Hotel* Visitors' Books 1869 -1936 has been published by Mrs Fiona Campbell whose family have owned the inn for many years. As can be imagined, there have been lots of interesting personalities accommodated here over the years. One entry in 1869 simply says 'Arthur'. He was HRH Prince Arthur William Patrick Albert, 1st Duke of Connaught and Strathearn 1850 – 1942, 3rd son of Queen Victoria. He was accompanied by his friend Colonel Elphinstone.

In 1870 the first recorded account of a climbing accident is noted: *"The kindness of Mr. and Mrs. Macdonald (the innkeepers) on the occasion of the sad accident on Scuir na Gillean, whereby Mr John Thom lost his life, will ever be gratefully remembered."*

(The Isle of Skye Mountain Rescue Team was set up in the early 1850s.)

One particular hotel guest, who accompanied Major G. L. Bruce of the Indian Army, Havildar Harkabir Thapa, a Gurka, better known as Herkia, set off from the door of the *Sligachan Hotel*, in bare feet, one fine day in 1899 and ran to the top of *Glamaig* and back, in just 55minutes. *Glamaig* is the highest and most northerly of the *Red Cuillin* and has two summits *An Coileach* to the north east and the higher point *Sgurr Mhairi*. This feat, although reliably timed and recorded as 37minutes up, and 18minutes down, was received with scepticism; many saying that it was not humanly possible, however 56 years later, George Rhodes went up in 37.5minutes and down in 19, almost equalling the record. For a number of years now, there is an annual commemorative event, and the new record, set in 1990 by Billy Rogers, stands at 46minutes and 2seconds.

Sheriff Alexander Nicolson was a regular visitor and was in the habit of writing an interesting comment or a verse, often in Gaelic. In 1872 he wrote; *"Mo bheannachd orra! Fhad's a bhith iad beo. Cha chaill Clann Domhnaill ann a seo an cliu!"* (My blessing be on them all their lives. (i.e. the hosts). The MacDonald Clan will not lose reputation (for hospitality) here!). In 1890 he wrote:

"Mo bheannachd air an tigh seo   "My blessings on this house
's na bheil ann.   and all that dwell within.
Fear'us bean an tighe   The kindly host and hostess
'us a chlann."   and their kin."

And again in 1891 part of his famous poem:

"Dunedin is queenly and fair –
None feels it more than I –
But in the prime of summer-time,
Give me the Isle of Skye!"

On census day 1881, my maternal grandfather, Duncan MacKinnon, unmarried, age 28, a master joiner from *Bracadale*, is recorded as present in the *Sligachan Hotel*. He was part of a team re-furbishing the inn for the coming season! His brother Neil, also a joiner, was here for the same purpose in 1900.

Otta Swire and Alexander Nicolson tell us that there was a much earlier (1375 or 1395) MacLeod-MacDonald battle near *Sligachan*. On this occasion the MacLeods forced the MacDonalds to retreat to their ships in Loch *Eynort*. The MacAskill coast watchers had been secretly at work, however, and had moored the MacDonald fleet in deep water, leading to the MacLeods gaining an overwhelming victory. Nicolson connects the 'Bloody Stone' in *Harta Corrie* with this particular battle.

In the *'Clarion'* newspaper, in the early 1950s, Ally Willie published a claim that gold had been successfully panned for in the *Kilmartin River* in *Trotternish*. The article prompted a letter to the editor which told that Mr. Coull of Lotts, Portree, in company with Lord Dunmore, had spoken with *'a titled gentleman'* whose wedding ring was made from gold found in the *Allt Dearg* burn, which runs down from the *Black Cuillin* to *Sligachan*. Perhaps it was this information which enticed speculative German geologists to spend time in the 1950s, searching for gold **and diamonds** in the *Sligachan* area!

We must now turn left on our homeward journey to Portree on the A87 main road through *Glen Varragill*. This valley benefits from superb views both to north and south. Towards *Trotternish* we have the spectacle of the *Storr* and the *'Old Man'*, always magnificent in good weather, but perhaps more atmospheric when mist swirls around them. To the south, the saw-toothed gabbro ridge of the Black Cuillin and the smooth, rounded granophyre of the Red Cuillin provide a fascinating contrast. More contrasts are apparent between the heathery, stock-grazed hillsides and the tall and maturing forestry plantations which have grown up, as I did, from the early 1950s. It is very salutary now to see the harvesting operation when it seems no time since I watched the planters! The forested blocks on our right were purchased by the Forestry Commission from the Braes Estate and had formed part of the hill grazing which had proved so controversial a hundred years before. For generations the Braes folk had made use of their sheilings, peat-banks and hill pasture, but in the 1870s Lord MacDonald leased the *Beinn Lì* grazings to a commercial sheep enterprise, over the heads of the resident crofters. Even when the lease was due for renewal in 1882, and the crofters offered to pay more than the sitting tenant, MacDonald's factor refused. Provoked by this injustice, the men released their animals onto the hill and some refused to pay croft rent until their claims were recognised. The Sheriff's officer duly arrived in their townships to serve eviction notices on the rent defaulters. The local populace gathered and forced the officer and his assistants to publicly burn the documents. The infuriated Sheriff William Ivory, unable to get sufficient Inverness officers, asked the Chief Constable of Glasgow to supply fifty policemen to quell the protests and arrest the leading agitators. When the arrogant Sheriff and his force reached Braes on a miserably wet April morning, they were met by about one hundred stick-wielding women and children, as most of the men were away at the fishing. The law-enforcers arrested the five rent-defaulters they had come for but, on their return towards Portree, were ambushed at *An Cumhang* (the narrow place), between hill and sea-cliff, and subjected to a hail of hard peats and stones. Several of the policemen suffered injuries but so also did the natives, *'one old woman being in a critical condition for several days'*. The five men Alexander and Malcolm Finlayson, Donald Nicolson, Peter MacDonald and James Nicolson, *Seumus Iain Oig* (my great-granduncle) were taken to the Portree jail overnight, prior to their trial at Inverness. They were convicted and fined. The fines were swiftly paid by the good citizens of Inverness and the men returned triumphantly as heroes to Skye next day. Following a further confrontation in October, the Braes crofters got their grazings back, at a reduced rental, and the rent strike came to an end. Further agitation continued in other parts of Skye, but eventually the publicity this *'last battle on British soil'* had generated, was sufficient to force Gladstone's Government to set up the Napier Commission of 1883.

Màiri Mhòr's poem *Beinn Lì* tells the story, publicises the victory and profusely thanks those who helped; other Skye crofters, city supporters and newspaper editors.

"Nuair thàinig e chiad uair
'S lethcheud 'aingeal' fo riaghladh,
Chuir e còignear an iarainn
Ann an crìochan Beinn Lì."

....

"'S ged tha 'n Cuilithionn is Glàmaig
Measg nam beanntan as àille,

"When he came the first time
With fifty 'angels' under his command
He put five men in irons
On the bounds of Ben Lee."

....

"Tho the Cuillin and Glamaig
Are 'mong hills the most noble,

Cha bhi 'n eachdraidh air a fàgail	History will find them
Ach aig sàiltean Beinn Lì."	Behind the heels of Ben Lee."
....	....
"Cuiribh litir le sòlas	"Send a letter of delight
Gu pàipear an Obain,	To the Oban Times,
A bha riamh ga ar còmhnadh	Which always supported us
Bhon là thòisich an strì."	From the start of the conflict."

As we drive north from *Sligachan* we pass on our left hand side, an area of flat marsh land called *Caiplach*. It was at *Loch Mòr na Caiplaich* that Pennant discovered a plant called pipewort, *piopan uisge (Eriocaulon septangulare aquaticum)*, which was illustrated by Moses Griffiths. It grows from little under-water rosettes and is very common on these hill lochs but is only occasionally found elsewhere on the island. Of course most of the plants on these peat-lands require to have an acid-tolerance and the commonest are eyebright, tormentil and other cinque-foils. From spring, the lesser celandines, dog violets, wood sorrel and wood anemones grow along the stream banks and it is in these days of warming sun that the primroses appear, followed, a few weeks later, by the wild hyacinths, which are English 'bluebells'. The bluebells of Scotland (rare in Skye), do not flower until August. Bog cotton shimmers in the breeze while the spear-like bog asphodels point heaven-wards from the wet ground, brightening the moorland after a long grey winter. The motor-bound traveller does not see these delights along *Glen Varragill*, but they are observed by those enjoying spring weather for peat-cutting. The peat-banks by the riverside belong to the Braes crofters and, although few now avail themselves of this fuel, it is a right for those with shares in the hill-grazing. Our family enjoyed this fresh-air task during the 1980s, but the road was so busy that loading bags of dried peat onto a trailer for transporting home, became too much of a hazard. Our most interesting wildlife sighting at this time was of an adder sunning itself on a drying peat!

Bird-life abounds, if you have the patience to observe.

Wheatear, stonechat, whinchat and the ever-present melodious skylark flit back and forth while you work.

Closer to Portree, by the riverside, we come on the remains of a lonely stone-walled homestead known as *Tobhta Lockhart*. There are still several families of this surname around the island, progeny of Lockharts who came to Skye from the border country along with the *Caoraich Mhòr* (the Big Sheep) in the late 19th Century.

As we approach Portree we can reflect on the journey we have made around the *Wings of the Wingèd Isle* and remind ourselves that there is still a large portion of Skye to be explored. Perhaps we will be able to do so in a third book, *'Beneath the Wings'*!

The Isle of Skye

By Andrew Dodds

"When wild winds fling against the door,
Beside the ingle blazing bright,
I like to sit alone, and pore
Upon my book of dreams at night:
A book that is a heritage
Thro' Celtic blood that I came by,
And fain I linger o'er the page
That tells me of the Isle of Skye.

I never sailed into Portree,
Nor found the road to Bracadale,
Adown the roaring of the gale,
I've seen the sheilings in the wild,
I've heard the plaintive moorbird's cry,
I've walked the gloaming as a child
Thro' elf-land in the Isle of Skye.

I've sat beside the glowing peat
O' winter nights, and heard the tales
They tell beyond the Sound of Sleat
When round the roof the wild wind rails;
I've heard the pipes out o'er the hill
On moonlit nights grow faint and die,
With glamorous tunes that rake and thrill
The hearts of men away in Skye.

Tho' I ne'er sail into Portree,
Nor find the road to Bracadale,
The windy nights will bring to me
The fairy folk to read the tale,
That's in the book that I've come by,
Of lands beyond the Sound of Sleat,
My mother's home, the Isle of Skye

The Gaelic Tree Alphabet

(the Gaelic Alphabet has 18 letters)

Ailm	Elm
Beithe	Birch
Coll	Hazel
Dair	Oak
Eadha	Aspen
Fèarn	Alder
Gort	Ivy
H (Uath)	Hawthorn
Iubhar	Yew
Luis	Rowan
Muin	Vine
Nùin	Ash
Oir	Gorse
P (Beithe bhog)	Downy Birch
Ruis	Elder
Suil	Willow
Teine	Furze
Ùr	Yew

Some Wildflowers to be seen in Skye

lus nam ban-sìth	foxglove
sòbhrach	primrose
broc na chuthaig	bluebell
neòinean	daisy
gealag-làir	snowdrop
buidheag	buttercup
achlais Challum Chille	St. John's wort
fraoch	heather
fraoch a' bhadain	bell-heather
cluaran	thistle
crois chuchulain	meadow-sweet

magairlean-beag nan dealan	lesser butterfly orchid
lus a' chrum chinn	daffodil
crom-lus	poppy
franach	Asphodel

Seasons of the Year

an t-earrach	spring
an samhradh	summer
am foghar	autumn
an geamhradh	winter

Some Mammals to be seen in and around Skye

broc	badger
cearban	basking shark
ialtag	bat
deilf	dolphin
sionach (madadh ruadh)	fox
mionc	mink
luchag	mouse
pèileag	porpoise
fiadh	red deer
earba	roe deer
dallag	shrew
feórag	squirrel
damh	stag
neas	stoat
famhalan	vole
easag	weasel
muc-mhara	whale
cat-fiadhaich	wildcat

Some Birds to be seen in Skye

caclach	arctic skua
steàrnan	arctic tern
gob-ceàrr	avocet
comhachag	barn owl
cathan	barnacle goose
muir-ghèadh	bean goose
lòn-dubh	blackbird
peacog	peacock
gealag bhuidhe	siskin
uiseag	skylark
sìolta bhreac	smew
naosg	snipe
eun an t-sneachda	snow bunting
omhachag bhan	snowy owl
smeòrach	song thrush
speireag	sparrowhawk
breacan sgiobalt	spotted flycatcher
druid	starling
clacharan	stonechat
luaireag	storm petrel
gobhlan-gaoithe	swallow
eala	swan
gobhlan-dubh	swift
cailleach oidhche	tawny owl
crann-lach	teal
riabhag-choille	tree pipit
snàigear	treecreeper
lach sgumanach	tufted duck
trilleachan beag	turnstone
riabhag fhraoich	twite
snagan allt	water rail
cànranach-dearg	waxwing
brù-geal	wheatear
eun-Bealltainn	whimbrel
clacharan an fhraoich	whinchat

Bibliography

Author	Title	Year	Place
Bassin E.	The Old Songs of Skye: Frances Tolmie & Her Circle	1977	London
Boswell J.	The Journal of a Tour to the Hebrides	1786	London
Cameron A.	The History and Traditions of The Isle of Skye	1871	Inverness
Cooper D.	Skye	1970	London
Coull J.R.	Fishing in Skye	2005	Aberdeen
Dempster A.	Skye 360	2003	Edinburgh
Gordon S.	The Charm of Skye : The Winged Isle	1929	London
Humble B.H.	The Songs of Skye : An Anthology	1934	Stirling
Humble B.H.	Tramping in Skye	1933	Edinburgh
Hunter J. & MacLean C.	Skye: The Island	1986	Edinburgh
Johnson S.	A Journey to the Western Isles of Scotland	1774	London
MacColl A.W.	Land, Faith & The Crofting Community	2006	Edinburgh
MacCulloch J.A.	The Misty Isle of Skye	1905	Edinburgh
Macdonald I. G.	Like a Bird on the Wing	2008	Guildford
MacDonald J.	Discovering Skye	1982	Duntulm
MacDonald J.	Flora Macdonald: Heroine of the Jacobite Cause	1989	Duntulm
MacDonald J.	A Short History of Crofting in Skye	1998	Duntulm

Macdonald M.	Skye Camanachd : A Century Remembered	1992	Portree
MacGregor A.A.	Over the Sea to Skye	1926	Edinburgh
MacGregor J.	In the Footsteps of Bonnie Prince Charlie	1988	London
MacKenzie W.	Old Skye Tales : Traditions, Reflections and Memories	1933	Culnacnoc
MacLean S.	From Wood to Ridge	1999	Edinburgh
MacLeod B.	Seventeenth Century Skye	1950	Inverness
MacLeod C.	The Cruel Clearance of Raasay	2007	Dunfermline
MacLeod J.	Banner in the West	2008	Edinburgh
MacPherson D.	Gateway to Skye	1946	Stirling
MacPherson G. W.	Traditional Stories from North West Skye	1984	Portree
MacPherson G. W.	Highland Myths and Legends	2001	Edinburgh
MacPherson M.	The Rough Road	1965	Edinburgh
MacSween A.	Skye	1990	Edinburgh
Marsh T.	The Isle of Skye : A Walker's Guide	1996	Milnthorpe
Martin Martin	A Description of the Western Isles of Scotland	1703	London
McGinn K.	Last of the Puffermen	2007	Glasgow
McMillan R.	Skye Birds	2005	Elgol
Meek D.	Mairi Mhor nan Oran	1997	Glasgow
Monro Sir D	Description of the Western Isles of Scotland called Hybrides	1774	Edinburgh
Murray C.W. & Birks	The Botanist in Skye	1974	Portree
Newton N.	Skye	1975	Newton Abbot

Nicolson A.	History of Skye (Revised 1994)	1995	Portree
Nicolson A.	Verses by Alexander Nicolson	1893	Edinburgh
Portree Local History Society	Sligachan Inn/Hotel Visitors' Books 1869 - 1936	2008	Portree
Sellar W.D.H. & MacLean A.	The Highland Clan MacNeacail (MacNicol)	1999	Waternish
Sillar F. C. & Meyler R.	Skye (Islands Series)	1973	Newton Abbot
Silver F.	The Skye Magazine	2006	Stornoway
Simpson J.W.	Cuillin of Skye Vols. I & II	1969	Edinburgh
Smith A.	A Summer in Skye	1865	London
Stephenson D. & Merrit J	Skye: A Lanscape Fashioned by Geology	2002	Edinburgh
Sterry P. & Press B.	Wildflowers of Britain and Europe	2004	London
Swire O. F.	Skye: The Island and its Legends	1952	Glasgow
Taylor L.S.	These Quiet Stones	1985	Broadford
Taylor S.	The Skye Revivals	2003	Chichester
Thomson D. S.	The Companion to Gaelic Scotland	1994	Glasgow
Tigh na Drochaid	Remembering Mairi Mhor	2007	Portree
Uncles C. J.	Last Ferry to Skye	1995	Ochiltree
Webster P. & H.	Isle of Skye : 40 Coast and Country Walks	2008	Bo'ness
Willis D.	The Story of Crofting in Scotland	1991	Edinburgh
Young J.	Short Walks on Skye	2006	Edinburgh
Yoxon P. & Yoxon G.	Guide to the Natural History of Skye	1987	Broadford

Printed in the United Kingdom by
Lightning Source UK Ltd., Milton Keynes
141673UK00001B/8/P